The NEW Fun Encyclopedia

The NEW Fun Encyclopedia

Volume 2   Parties and Banquets

E. O. Harbin
revised by
Bob Sessoms

ABINGDON PRESS

Nashville

THE NEW FUN ENCYCLOPEDIA

VOLUME II. PARTIES AND BANQUETS

Copyright © 1940 by Whitmore & Smith; renewed 1968 by Mary Elizabeth Harbin Standish and Thomas Harbin. Revised edition copyright © 1984 by Abingdon Press.

Library of Congress Cataloging in Publication Data

(Revised for vol. 2)
HARBIN, E. O. (Elvin Oscar), 1885–
  The new fun encyclopedia.
  Rev. ed. of: The fun encyclopedia. © 1940
  Bibliography: v. 1, p.
  Includes index.
  Contents: v. 1. Games— v. 2. Parties and Banquets.
  1. Amusements—Collected works. 2. Games—Collected works. 3. Entertaining—Collected works.
  I. Harbin, E. O. (Elvin Oscar), 1885–1955. Fun encyclopedia. II. Sessoms, Bob. III. Title
  GV1201.H383   1983   794   83-2818
  ISBN 0-687-27755-8 (v. 2)

0-687-27754-X (v. 1)
0-687-27756-6 (v. 3)
0-687-27757-4 (v. 4)
0-687-27758-2 (v. 5)
0-687-27759-0 (set)

MANUFACTURED BY THE PARTHENON PRESS AT NASHVILLE, TENNESSEE, UNITED STATES OF AMERICA

CONTENTS

INTRODUCTION

*T*he social climate of a past era was captured by E. O. Harbin. I have attempted to capture the social climate of this era by the addition of more modern material, while retaining that which is timeless. My hope is that you will enjoy not only E. O. Harbin's activities, but those of today. May your mind be stimulated to reach into this vast resource and create your own fun-filled party, banquet, or fellowship. Remember that by keeping the enjoyment of your guests foremost in your planning, you will be better able to provide a pleasurable experience in a social setting.

BOB SESSOMS

1

SOCIAL RECREATION

The words *social recreation* automatically bring to mind parties. However, social recreation also includes banquets, fellowships, receptions and teas, open houses, fairs and carnivals, breakfasts, brunches, lunches, dinners, picnics, and even coffee breaks. Social recreation can be defined as *people interacting with one another in a social setting.* And it is for all ages.

A person who directs social recreation should consider some important guidelines. Although these do not necessarily guarantee success, they do provide a way to achieve the goals of social recreation: that the guests not only enjoy the experience of togetherness, but become better people because of the event.

THE SOCIAL DIRECTOR

The social director has the overall responsibility for coordinating the plans to insure the guests an enjoyable experience. The director should be aware of the social needs of the group involved and try to meet those needs with wholesome activities. The atmosphere of the event and attitude of the participants lie within the control of the social director.

This person enlists subcommittees, estimates budget needs, coordinates the total planning, and evaluates the finished product.

The more people enlisted to help with the event, the more enthusiasm will be generated. However, the committee should not be overloaded with nonproductive individuals.

THE COMMITTEES

Steering Committee—This committee is composed of the social director, who acts as chairperson to coordinate the various aspects of the event and delegate responsibilities; and the chairpersons of the following subcommittees.

Publicity—This chairperson is to enlist talented, artistic, creative people to design and produce publicity that will promote enthusiasm for the social event. This committee should work closely with other committees to communicate the real spirit of the event. *All* the facts should be included in the publicity—date, time, place, dress code, cost (if any), and age factor.

Program—With a selected group of socially minded people, this chairperson should plan the program, activities, and/or entertainment for the event. There should be a detailed schedule ready in plenty of time for the decorating committee to carry out its function. This chairperson should also work hand in hand with the social director in leading the program of activities.

Decorations—After the theme has been determined, after the program of activities has been decided upon, and after the promotion has gone into effect, the decorations chairperson should assemble a committee of committed workers to decorate (and undecorate) for the function. Decorations should be based on the theme of the event.

Refreshments—A person skilled in the art of creative food should serve as this chairperson. This committee should work closely with the others to coordinate suitable refreshments. The food should complement the theme of the social.

Transportation—If transportation is needed (for senior adults, children, younger youth, or anyone) this chairperson should enlist qualified drivers and vehicles for the occasion.

GUIDELINES

In any social event, planning is of the utmost importance. Good leaders will plan a detailed strategy to accomplish the goals of the event. Here is a list to consider.

Plan with a purpose. Discover the social needs of the group involved. Direct the event to meet those needs. Choose activities wisely.

Know the facility. Where will the event take place? Will it accommodate the activities, decorations, and size of the group? If out-of-doors, consider the weather. What about safety? Are there any hazards that may cause problems?

Know the group. What is the age, sex, social makeup, and physical limitation of the participants? Consider their physical abilities and their ability to understand and follow instructions.

Be prepared. Always have more games or entertainment than may be needed. It is better to be overprepared than underprepared. However, be sensitive to the group. If an activity is not catching on, switch to another. Do not overplay. BEGIN ON TIME! END ON TIME! STOP AT THE PEAK OF FUN!

Do not force participation, but encourage it.

Do not embarrass any guest.

Keep all activities in good and proper taste. Be selective in choosing activities. Try not to offend anyone.

Emphasize the fun aspect of the activity, not the competitive aspect. Have a variety of activities planned.

Set up before the event. Do not wait until the last moment to decorate or set up for games. Allow plenty of time for emergencies or last minute changes.

Have something for the early arriver to do.

Greet the guests in a friendly and unrushed manner. Name tags will help identify everyone.

Keep a positive, light-hearted attitude and exhibit enthusiasm during the event. Be sensitive to the group.

As a Game Leader—

1. Stand where people can see and hear you. Examples:

In a circle

In a line

More than one line

For relays

2. Use your normal speaking voice when giving instructions. If needed, use a public address system. In gaining the attention of the group, use a whistle, bell, or whatever you prefer.

3. Have the guests gather into the formation required for the activity.

4. Tell them the name of the game or activity.

5. Share the instructions of the game, then *demonstrate* to the group. Have a trial run before beginning. Give ample opportunity for questions.

6. Be enthusiastic!

7. Stop at the peak of fun! Do not play until everyone is bored.

SOME QUESTIONS TO ANSWER

What group is involved in the social event?

What are the age differences? What is the ratio of males to females?

What is the purpose of the party? What do you hope to accomplish?

What does the group like to do?

What is the facility for the event? Is it conducive to this type of activity? Does it satisfy the requirements for space? How many people will it accommodate?

How much time is allotted for the event? Can all that is planned be accomplished?

PUBLICITY

Communicating the social event to the public is essential. Without people, there is no social. In the publicity, answer these questions: Who? What? When? Where? Whether in a newspaper or on a poster, the answers will provide the needed information.

Publicity should be attractive, eye catching, and bold. A good method is to develop a color theme and carry it throughout, in publicity as well as in decorations. Do not be too wordy, and use easy-to-read words and letters. A symbol, design, or logo might enhance promotion; it could be used on each piece of publicity. So, use key words boldly; repeat a color theme throughout; and use a symbol or design to identify the event.

An ordinary poster does not always communicate unless it has an unusual, eye-catching appeal. So make the posters unique. Fabric, large (refrigerator) boxes, spotlights, glitter, large cutout letters that cover an entire wall, mobiles that hang from the ceiling, doorknob leaflets, words on stairsteps—these are a few suggestions for carrying out the promotion a little more creatively than just writing a felt-tip pen message on white poster board. It is essential to have good publicity.

Social recreation may take many forms, but in each, people are needed to plan, work, communicate, and create a successful social experience for those who participate. May your creative mind adjust, adapt, or re-create the suggestions that follow. May you and your guests enjoy the spiritual refreshment of a successful social recreation experience.

FUN WITH BANQUETS

Any mood, from formal to informal, can be set for a banquet. A banquet is a sit-down meal, with a program provided by any of the following: toastmaster, speaker, entertainer (magician, comic, singer, ventriloquist, mime or chalk-talk expert), other entertainment (choir, drama, puppets, slides, motion picture), or simply soft music.

POINTERS

A good theme helps.

Decorations in keeping with the theme add interest.

Informality, spontaneity, surprise, variety, fun, and good fellowship are basic necessities for success.

If speeches are included in the program, they should be snappy, brief, and a happy combination of the humorous and serious.

Check carefully on the probable attendance, at least the day before the banquet. Don't guess. Know.

Check all arrangements carefully.

Organize so that the work can be distributed. There should be a steering committee and subcommittees on program, menu, decorations, table arrangements, and attendance.

TEN COMMANDMENTS FOR THE TOASTMASTER

1. Plan carefully what thou wouldst do. They who trust to the last moment for inspiration will find that moment a fickle and faithless friend.

2. Allow no moss to grow under thy feet as the banquet getteth under way. Verily, a slow-moving banquet is a vexation to the spirit.

3. Thou shalt not feel it necessary to expound on the subject before or after each speaker's speech. Blessed is the toastmaster who knoweth how to be brief.

4. Thou shalt not endeavor to embarrass persons on the program by telling allegedly humorous stories about them. Blessed is the toastmaster who can be smart without being a smartaleck. And verily it is said that they who sling mud do lose ground.

5. Thou shalt inform those on the program of the limits of time, and then thou shalt see that these limits are observed. For verily, there is a difference between time and eternity, and a speaker whose terminal facilities are poor needeth to be sidetracked.

6. Thou shalt pay honor to whom honor is due. For truly, words of appreciation fitly spoken are "like apples of gold in pictures of silver."

7. Thou shalt repolish thy old jokes and endeavor to dig up a few new ones. For forsooth, an old joke many times retold doth become a pain in the neck.

8. Thou shalt exude enthusiasm with the greatest of ease. Nothing so troubleth the spirit of banqueteers as a toastmaster who hath no spizerinktum.

9. Thou shalt know the facts about the persons thou dost introduce—who they are, from whence they come, what they do and have done. Thou shalt then tell it briefly without fulsome flattery. A poor introduction is a grievance to the flesh.

10. Thou shalt bring the program to a fitting conclusion. A good climax is to be desired more than a confused

banquet crowd which looketh bewildered and sayeth, "Well, is it over?"

They who hear and do these things shall bless the land in which they live.

A TOASTMASTER'S POEM

Whatever troubles Adam had,
No one in days of yore
Could say, when he told a joke,
"I've heard that one before."

TREASURE HUNT BANQUET

Publicity—Information sheets may be sent to each organization, with a drawing such as a treasure chest in one corner, and a skull and crossbones in the other; in the center could be these lines from Robert Louis Stevenson:

If sailor takes to sailor tunes,
    Storm and adventure, heat and cold,
If schooners, islands, and maroons,
    And buccaneers and buried gold,
And all the old romance, retold
    Exactly in the ancient way,
Can please, as me they pleased of old,
    The wiser youngsters of today:

So be it, and fall on!

Decorations—These are very important and will add immensely to the motif if properly carried out. Black and red is a good combination for crepe-paper streamers. Large cutout pirate heads can be used. Imitation gold money (chocolate candy wrapped in foil) can be scattered on the tables, representing pieces of eight. One or two ship models should be placed on each table. The speakers' table can be cleverly arranged with a large mirror for water and a small sand island, on which may be placed a few trees and small pirate figures near a ship model.

Menu—The menu may be labeled The Treasure Chest and include such items as Pirates' Delight, Treasure Island, Candied Skeleton, Doubloon Salad, Fifteen Men on a Dead Man's Chest, Pie-rates' Cove, Yo-ho-ho, Skulls, Crossbones. Shrimp Creole* would be a good main dish.

Program—The program may be called the Log; an invocation titled Bon Voyage. Group singing may be listed as Mutiny of the Crew, using such improvised ditties as these:

> Sing, sing, the pirates' chant:
>   "Who will be the victim?
>   Who will be the victim?"
> Yell as though you've "seen a hant"!
> Come and join our pirate band.
>
> (*Tune:* "Hail, Hail the Gang's All Here")

> Sail, sail, sail your ships,
>   Grandly o'er the sea,
> Merrily, merrily, merrily, merrily,
>   Pirates all are we.
>
> (*Tune:* "Row, Row, Row Your Boat")

Important personages may be introduced under the heading Ships Ahoy! Suggested titles for talks: "Latitude and Longitude," "SOS," "Powder and Arms," "Ships That Pass in the Night." Musical numbers such as "The Volga Boatman" and "The Road to Mandalay" may be chosen.

*Throughout this volume, starred menu items refer to recipes in the Recipe chapter.

GEORGE WASHINGTON'S BIRTHDAY BANQUET
A Progressive Dinner Party

Invitation Next Friday night at six o'clock,
To _____'s we all will flock,
To celebrate Great George
And the Immortal Tree,
His gift to all posterity.

February 22

First Home

Game: Be Truthful. Make two sets of numbers. Give each player a number from one set. The leader keeps the other set in a hat. The leader starts the game by asking a question such as "Who has the biggest ears?" then pulls any number out of the hat. The player who has that number stands up and says, "I have." Then that player asks a question to be answered by the next player whose number is called by the leader.

Course: Fruit cocktail or Soup.

Second Home

Game: Cherry Race. A bowl is filled with cherries (or cranberries) and each player thrusts a hand, palm down, into the bowl to see how many cherries can be picked up on the back of the hand. Without spilling a cherry, the player must circle the room three times in two minutes. If two or more people have similar scores, they continue to compete until one is victor. Crowd can be divided into sides, the side having the largest number of cherries being the winner.

Course: Hot roast-beef sandwiches or Stew Beef Casserole.*

Third Home

Game: Declaring Independence. Give a copy of the following list to each player:

1. I declare myself free of _____
2. Because _____
3. And I resolve to _____
4. At _____
5. On _____

Each person fills in the first blank, then folds over the answer and passes the paper to the next player. After all papers have been passed five times and all questions answered, have the declarations read aloud.

Course: Baked beans, rye bread, relish.

Fourth Home

Game: Cherry Cube. Make cubes with the letters C-H-E-R-R-Y on them. You will need six cubes for each game. A player who turns up C-H gets 5 points; for C-H-E, 10; and so on. The complete word scores an extra 5 points.

Course: Vegetable salad.

Fifth Home

Game: A Famous Washington. Give out the following verses to be guessed. Each verse describes a famous Washington.

I threw a dollar across the river;
I cut down a cherry tree;
But that anyone would remember these
Just never occurred to me. (George Washington)

My place in the sun
Is a very small one;
I loved him, that's all,
And our two lives were one. (Martha Washington)

I might have lived and died unknown,
Had not fate given me a son;
The cherry tree belonged to me,
And that is why I'm famed, you see.
(Washington's father)

I make no claim to wealth or fame,
Nor to position high;
I only taught him 'twas a shame
For gentlemen to lie. (Washington's mother)

They come and go within my gates,
The senators, diplomats, presidents;
I'm the center of politics, of nations' fates,
And many are my residents. (Washington, D.C.)

I am the largest Washington
That ever bore that name,
So my native sons and daughters
To this glory have a claim. (Washington state)

I lift my granite grandeur high,
Telling of fame that will not die;
Bearing aloft in rain or sun
The deathless name of Washington.
(Washington Monument)

Though my race was not the same,
I too bore the illustrious name,
And I tried to teach my people
That hard labor is no shame. (Booker T. Washington)

They gave me his name,
Hoping it would bring fame;
But my only claim to glory
Is that I could tell a story. (Washington Irving)

Course: Cherry pie a la mode.

The banquet can end with the singing of patriotic songs.

FISHERS OF MEN

Publicity—Using construction paper, cut out several different sizes of boats like those used in the days of Christ. Glue these on poster board and print *Fishers of Men,* with the date, time, and place of the event. To really capture attention, place a small boat with a mast and sail, depicting a fishing boat, in a conspicuous place. On the sail, inscribe with tempera paint the words *Fishers of Men Banquet.* Fishnets in the boat will add to the decor.

Decorations—The head table area can serve as a focal point. Using a very large piece of cardboard, cut out a side view of a fishing boat and paint it to look like a boat. The mast can be centered between two tables. The sail should remain tied up. In front of the vessel, construct a dock using logs and pieces of wood. Rope should be tied around the logs to give the effect of a boat dock (see sketch).

Tables can be covered with pieces of fishnet and decorated with driftwood, sea shells, and baskets of hard rolls that will serve as part of the meal. Paper cutouts of fish can be placed on the tables, and hurricane lamps could also be included. The walls can be covered with large cutouts of fish or large mural drawings of Christ and his disciples fishing. Fishnets also could be hung on the walls.

Menu   Clam Chowder* or Seafood Gumbo*
Fish fillets
Coleslaw   French fries
Hush puppies or hard rolls
Sherbet
Coffee/Iced tea

Program—The speakers' theme could be "Reaching Others for Christ." Printed programs could be cut in the shape of a boat.

STORYTELLER'S BANQUET

Everybody enjoys a good story. Consider a storyteller's banquet. Before the event, audition those who wish to participate by listening to their stories. It is best to set aside one day for auditions. Enlist several persons to serve as a panel of judges. Be sure to have a timekeeper.

In the publicity announcing the auditions, list the types of stories that qualify for this type of affair. This should be done well in advance so individuals can practice, memorize, or make up interesting tales. Some senior adults memorized stories in their younger years. Encourage these people to try out for this event.

Publicity—Posters could feature a person telling a story. Have an open book with "Once upon a time . . . ," or have the poster look like a page of a book, relating facts about the banquet. Or fold a large piece of cardboard into the shape of a book, print the information on the cardboard, and place it in a conspicuous place.

Decorations—The head table should be reserved for the participants. A speaker's stand with microphone (if available) will help create an atmosphere for these speakers. Have a pitcher of fresh cold water and a glass for each speaker in case of dry throat. Place a large bouquet of flowers in front of the speaker's stand.

Arrange the other tables so that everyone can see the speaker. Decorate the tables with floral arrangements and various storybooks set upright. An array of candles could also set the mood for this banquet. Have soft music playing during the meal. Enlist someone to play various selections on the piano, or use records. If some people have old 78 rpm records, you might have them bring some.

Menu   Baked ham or Chicken Casserole*
Candied yams   Broccoli Casserole*
Gelatin Salad*
Rolls
Lemon Pie*
Coffee/Tea

Program—Have a master of ceremonies preside over the program. Before the banquet, have each speaker fill out a brief biographical sketch, humorous if possible. This will help the MC introduce each speaker. Begin with the humorous stories and lead up to the more serious ones. Conclude the evening with a story that emphasizes a spiritual quality. Have musical numbers between stories, if time allows.

Adapted from Bob and Carolyn Sessoms, *52 Complete Recreation Programs for Senior Adults* (Nashville: Convention Press, 1979), pp. 41-42. Used by permission.

APRIL FOOL BANQUET

Decorations—Toy balloons, cutout clowns, clown dolls, etc.

Menu—Give the articles on the menu names that are appropriate, but do not disclose their identity. Have surprises in the menu, perhaps Beef and Corn Casserole*. Be sure all are palatable. It would not be a great deal of fun to bite into cotton biscuits or soap confections. For instance, beside each plate there could be a cup and saucer with the cup turned upside down. Everyone will think this is intended for coffee, but when guests lift the cup they find under it a gelatin fruit salad, or something of that sort.

Program—The chairman should introduce someone as toastmaster. That person should immediately arise and protest that there has been some mistake; that it is true they had talked with him about it, but he had not agreed to serve. He suggests that John Smith is the one who was elected. John Smith gets up and also begs to be excused, saying there is some misunderstanding. He insists that Arthur Jones was to be toastmaster, and so it goes until they finally find someone.

The toastmaster, who finally has been corralled, introduces the various items on the program. However, nobody does what the toastmaster announces they are to do. For instance, if it is announced that Miss Brown will play a violin solo, Miss Brown plays a piano solo. Someone is introduced to sing and instead, gives a reading, or a poem, or a dramatic skit. Another is introduced to make a talk on some announced subject, but instead of talking, sings, and so on. Much will depend upon the toastmaster, who proceeds with the program as if nothing were amiss.

MAGIC BANQUET

The Magic Mirror makes not nor unmakes,
Charms none to sleep nor any from sleep wakes;
It only giveth back the thing it takes.

Menu   Roast turkey and dressing
                      Cranberry sauce
          Candied sweet potatoes   Peas
              Pineapple and cheese salad
                        Hot rolls
          Ice cream   Coconut Cake*
                         Coffee

You will not need to be a magician to make the food
disappear.

Program—*Toastmaster and Chief Magician:* This program will be valuable particularly if your toastmaster
knows something about magic. However, it is not necessary for the toastmaster to be skilled in legerdemain.
Tricks of magic would be appropriate. The toastmaster

may pull the program out of a hat or look into a crystal ball. Thus group singing, special music, and stunts may be introduced.

Address or Discussion Topic—"If I Had a Magic Wand."

```
???????????????????????
??                     ??
??      SINCE THIS IS   ??
??    A MAGIC BANQUET   ??
??         THE          ??
??   TOASTMASTER WILL   ??
??   PULL THE PROGRAM   ??
??    OUT OF THE HAT    ??
??                     ??
???????????????????????
```

STAR FLIGHT

Publicity—All around the building, post drawings of spaceships flying among the various planets. Helium-filled balloons placed at different levels overhead can give the appearance of planets. A message written on the balloons can convey the banquet information.

Decoration—The decorating committee will need to do research on this particular banquet. Members can use their creative imagination. Much will depend upon the latest achievements in space technology. This is but one suggestion for decorating.

By contacting N.A.S.A. (National Aeronautics and Space Administration) in Washington, D.C., slides or video tapes of current space achievements might be obtained. Use a rear projection screen to show slides or tapes as part of the decorations. Appropriate music and/or narration will enhance the program before the banquet begins. Table centerpieces may consist of rectangular boxes covered in red foil, with white letters reading *Launch Pad 1,* etc. On top of each box, place a replica of a space shuttle or rocket booster, or the latest in space vehicles. Other decorations can be space-related posters, model satellites attached to the ceiling, or replicas of the solar system. The printed program can be designed in the shape of a rocket ship.

Menu   *Space Shuttle Buffet*
Sliced ham and roast beef
Baked potato   Lima Bean Casserole*
Marinated vegetable salad
(tomato wedges, sliced cucumbers and bell peppers in
Italian dressing)
Rolls
Strawberry Layer Cake*
Beverage

Program—This can be a kick-off for a campaign, for raising a budget, or it can be an ordinary social event.

RUBE'S RURAL REUNION

Menu   Baked ham   Hard-boiled eggs
Turnip greens   Corn on the cob
Potato salad   Sliced tomatoes
Corn bread
Apple pie
Coffee

Program—Designate tables as communities such as Slocum Gap, Pomona Junction, etc. Appoint some "squires" as toastmasters. The squires preside very informally. From time to time one rises and introduces a "speaker." For instance, Squire "Beet" Miller would introduce "Roasnear" North to speak on "Nubbins or Full Ears"; or "Hayseed" Gwinner, to speak on "Make Hay While the Sun Shines." Other program features could be The Bullfrog Sextette, banjo pickers, bird imitations, a corn-husking contest.

Programs could be cut into watermelon-slice shapes.

WINTER WONDERLAND

Publicity—Publicize this event with answers to the questions What is it? Where is it? When is it? Who is it for? How much does it cost? A small branch with twigs could be painted white and adorned with small blinking white lights. From the branches, hang pieces of blue construction paper with the pertinent information written in white ink.

Decorations—Using the white tree with blinking lights as a key to the theme, line the room with trees. At the base of each tree and on some limbs, place white cotton, or spray artificial snow. Silver icicles will add to the wintery look. A styrofoam snowman, mannequins dressed in wintery outfits, a sled or two, a sleigh, and/or skis could accentuate the theme. Blue floodlights would create an atmosphere of winter.

The tables could have white tablecloths with a blue ribbon stretched down the center, and blue napkins. Blue candles set among pine needles sprayed with artificial snow would add just the right touch.

The program could be printed with blue ink on white paper, with the outline of a leafless tree or a large snowflake.

Menu   Roast beef
        Broccoli Casserole*   Potatoes with gravy
                    Gelatin salad
                    Blueberry muffins
                    Lemon Pie*
                    Beverage

Program—A choir could sing songs related to winter: "Winter Wonderland," "Silver Bells," "Jingle Bells."

CIRCUS WORLD

Publicity—Make posters resembling circus posters, with wild animals, trapeze artists, clowns, elephants, etc. Include the date, time, place, and cost in large letters. Post these in conspicuous places.

Decorations—The dining area can resemble a circus tent. Alternating strips of red and white or yellow crepe paper can be draped at the entrance. A "barker," dressed in costume and carrying a cane, can announce the events of the evening from a stand. Large drawings of The Strongest Man in the World, The Bearded Lady, The Clowns, etc., can be placed by the entrance and around the room.

Arrange the tables in a large rectangle, leaving the center of the room for the "center ring." Circus music can be playing as the guests arrive. A tent can be constructed by attaching a wire lengthwise down the center of the room. Two more wires may be hung slightly lower on each side of the center wire to allow crepe-paper strips to be draped over them (see illustration). Those who serve the tables can be dressed as clowns.

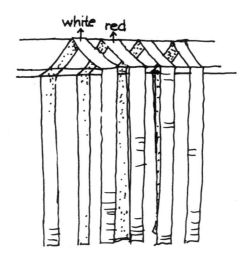

Menu

Ringmaster's beef
Pretty lady's beans   Muscleman's potatoes
Barker's Reception Salad*
Animal Trainer's Rolls*
Clown's Delight Impossible Pie*
Sideshow beverages

Program—The program should present a circus-type entertainment. The Strong Man may not be able to pick up the 5,000 pound weight (consisting of two large balloons attached to a stick), but the Clown might. Other entertainment might include a juggler, a magician, a tumbling act, clown stunts, trained dogs, or a variety of skits.

HILLBILLY BASH

Publicity—In the promotion, inform everyone to dress very casually—blue jeans, flannel shirt, boots—a country-western look.

Decorations—The stage area might boast a large yellow harvest moon on a royal blue backdrop. Stacks of hay bales, an old outhouse, a split-rail fence, and an old wagon wheel will enhance the area. Red-checkered paper tablecloths and napkins, and lanterns or hurricane lamps can adorn the tables, with colorful Indian corn and gourds.

Menu
Country ham
Candied yams   Green peas
Corn Bread*
Pig Pickin' Cake*
Iced tea in a fruit jar

Program—A country band, a guitar player who sings country music, a fruit-jar band, a comedian, a quartet, or a fiddle player could set a festive mood for this country gathering.

SHOWBOAT BANQUET

Publicity—Promotion should announce that the Showboat's A-Comin', and should include the time, date, place, and cost.

Decorations—If possible, construct the front or side of a showboat. If unable to do that, a large drawing or painting will suffice. Logs or pieces cut from telephone poles can give the appearance of pilings along a dock, with ropes to give the appearance of a boat tied to the dock. Greenery can add to the river bank appearance. A large drawing of a southern plantation, a gazebo, bales of cotton—all can add to the showboat theme.

Tables can include Magnolia leaves and blooms—real, artificial, or cut from construction paper. Candles are a natural at this banquet.

Menu   Fried chicken
Mashed potatoes   Green beans
Apple pie
OR
If you are daring, ham hocks, turnip greens, black-eyed peas, and Mississippi Mud.*

Program—An old-fashioned melodrama, a banjo player, a vaudeville-type comedy team, a soprano or a barbershop quartet singing Stephen Foster music would create a night to remember.

A SMALL, SMALL WORLD

This banquet could serve as a Valentine's Day celebration for a variety of groups: children, families with children, youth, adults, or older adults. If for a church occasion, it could focus on missions.

Publicity—Promotion could consist of a globe surrounded by hearts, dolls dressed in costumes of various countries, with posters giving the date, time, and place.

Decorations—The decorations make this banquet. Cut from brown paper, large gingerbread-looking dolls can be hung around the walls near the ceiling. Flags from other countries can be placed around the room. In a gymnasium, these dolls and flags can be hung from the running track. Cartoon-type drawings of children in costumes of various countries can adorn the walls, in place of or in addition to the gingerbread dolls. Large (33-inch) helium-filled balloons with small baskets tied to them can float at different heights in the room, if the ceiling is high enough, giving the appearance of hot-air balloons.

Carvings, fans, and souvenirs from countries around the world can be placed on the tables; dolls or small mannequins of children dressed in costumes can serve as centerpieces; red and white carnations in vases, or candy, suckers, hearts, and valentines can be used.

The front of the room could be decorated with mannequins from department stores or animated dolls in costumes (like those seen in store windows at Christmastime). A stage area can be decorated with a rainbow and the words *It's a Small, Small World*. During the meal Walt Disney tunes can brighten up the festive occasions.

Menu   Turkey and dressing
       Sweet potatoes   Asparagus Casserole*
              Cherry gelatin salad
                 Baked apple
                  Beverage

Program—The program might consist of a puppet show, children singing, a men's or women's barbershop quartet, a couple singing music for children, handbells, or a children's piano concert. If there is a speaker, the message should emphasize the closeness of the world and the way love can bring people together.

AN EVENING IN ROME

Publicity—Promotion could be written in Roman script (such as a V for a U) and illustrated with cartoon characters of Roman soldiers or emperors.

Decorations—Mannequins or dolls can be dressed in sheets or, if available from department stores, the white mannequins that look like statues can be used. These, along with white columns and greenery (fake bushes or trees), can transform the room into a Roman garden. A river of blue crepe paper could be laid throughout the room, with a small bridge to grace it. Artificial or real fountains can add to the decorations.

Menu—The bill of fare could be written in pig latin.

Menu	*Enuma*
Juice	Uiceja
Spaghetti	Paghettisa
Tossed Salad	Ossedta Aladsa
Bread	Readba
Banana Torte*	Ananaba Orteta

Program—The printed program could also be written in pig latin. Poetry could be read in pig latin or circus-type acts could perform. For an evening in Rome, an opera might be performed. *The Grasshopper Opera* would be a good one.

CAMELOT

Everyone enjoys hearing or reading about those days of princesses, knights in shining armor, castles, and dragons. King Arthur's Camelot has inspired a musical and a movie, and allows one to dream of days long ago.

Publicity—Large posters depicting castles, knights on horses, or fire-breathing dragons can capture the attention of your target group. The guests may dress in costumes of the period.

Decorations—Here the imagination can run wild. The door to the dining hall can be decorated to look like the entrance to a castle. Cut a large piece of cardboard and paint it to look like a stone wall. A make-believe moat can be created with blue crepe paper. A drawbridge of planks nailed together should have large chains or rope connecting it to the wall.

The dining hall can be set up like a large banquet hall. The walls here can also appear to be of stone, with stained-glass windows added to the cardboard. Brightly colored flags can be placed around the room or hung from the ceiling. Coats of arms may be painted, and drawings of full suits of armor may also adorn the walls. Locate a large fireplace with fake fire behind the main table. Arrange the tables so there is a large space for entertainment. The king and queen should have a throne to sit upon while viewing the program. Tables may have candles and plenty of brightly colored flowers. Waiters and waitresses can be dressed in clothes of the period.

Menu—A feast fit for a king could be prepared—a roast pig, complete with apple in mouth. A more practical bill of fare:

Barbecued pork

Baked beans   Pan-fried potatoes

Tossed salad

Danish Puff*

Beverage

Program—As in the days of King Arthur, minstrels, string quartets, circus acts (juggling, tumbling, gymnastics), puppets, mime can be a part of the festivities.

BREAKFAST IN THE PARK

In the spring, or in the fall of the year when the colors of nature are painting the landscape, have a breakfast in the park. If you live on the coast, have the cookout on the beach in the early morning. This event takes coordination.

Decorations—Eating utensils, plates, napkins, salt and pepper, butter, etc., must be obtained and tables set. There is no need to decorate extensively for this type of cookout, but bouquets of spring flowers or arrangements of fall leaves, depending upon the season, would be appropriate.

Menu—Food must be selected and prepared. Cooking gear—grills and/or charcoal, ice chests, and so on—must be obtained. Suggestions for the menu: eggs (scrambled, omelettes of all types, hard-boiled), a meat (bacon, sausage, Canadian bacon, ham), bread (toast, biscuits, pastry, Ripple Coffeecake*, pancakes, french toast), hashed-brown potatoes, fresh fruit, beverage (juice, milk, tea, coffee, hot chocolate).

Program—Obtain a speaker who can bring a very inspirational message concerning God's creation and the hope of a new dawn.

PROGRESSIVE LUNCHEON

Reservations for this activity are a must in order to prepare enough food. A bus would be best for transportation. Otherwise, drive in cars, but do not go in a caravan. Give each driver a map showing the routes to each location. Allow enough time to drive safely.

Select three homes to host the appetizer, salad, and dessert courses. The main course can be prepared and served at the church or other facility. Have everyone meet at a designated time and place, and leave for the first course from there.

First Home

Game: The host or hostess places a name tag on the back of each guest with the name of a famous person in history, a movie star, or a comic strip character. Each guest pairs with another and they ask each other yes or no questions about who they are supposed to be. When most guests have guessed who they represent, serve the appetizer and enjoy casual conversation.

Course: Juice, carrot and celery sticks, crackers, and Cucumber Dip*.

Second Home

Game: Have everyone sit in a circle. Someone chosen to be IT goes into the center of the circle and is blindfolded. Everyone changes places and one person, selected by the leader, leaves the room. IT removes the blindfold and looks around to see who is missing. If IT guesses correctly, the person who left the room becomes IT. Otherwise, IT gets another chance to guess. Play for just a few minutes, then enjoy the salad.

Course: Use your creativity in creating a tossed or gelatin salad. Try Reception Salad* or Frozen Banana Salad*.

Church or Other Facility

Game: Have the tables separated, with four to six people at a table. Be sure that each table has pencil and paper and the same number of people. Each group should select someone who can add well to serve as statistician, and follow these instructions.
  1. Add everyone's age together and obtain a total for your group.

2. Add one point for each child each family in your group has.
3. Add two points for each grandchild each family has.
4. Add five points for each great-grandchild; ten points for each great-great-grandchild.
5. Add one point for each state the people in the group have lived in.
6. With January as one point, February as two, and so on throughout the calendar year, total the number of birthday points for your table.
7. Add a point for each person who is wearing a piece of handmade clothing or jewelry.
8. Score a point for each pet owned (fish not included).
9. Add a point for each different brand of watch in the group.
10. For each letter of each given name, add a point. Example: Fredricka has 9 letters, so 9 points are added.

Total all the points. The table with the most wins.

Course: Tomato-smothered Steak*, green beans, scalloped potatoes, bread, beverage.

Third Home

Course: Serve scoops or alternate layers of orange and lime sherbet, with sugar cookies.

Devotional: The occasion may be closed with a brief devotional. Take this time to thank God for the meal and the fellowship.

Adapted from Bob and Carolyn Sessoms, *52 Complete Recreation Programs for Senior Adults* (Nashville: Convention Press, 1979), pp. 44-45. Used by permission.

HOMECOMING IDEAS

You are cordially invited to attend the Homecoming Celebration of Cedar Creek Church on Sunday, August _____, 19___.

Services will be held at 11:00 A.M. Dinner on the grounds will be
served immediately after the service. Bring enough food for your
family, plus one. The church will provide the beverage. At 1:00,
we will assemble at the cemetery for singing and the annual
homecoming sermon. The offering will go toward upkeep of the
cemetery.

Sound familiar? This traditional announcement is
meaningful to the members, guests, and former members
of Cedar Creek, and to those of countless other churches
throughout the land. Homecoming is a time of fellowship,
reunion, and remembering. We hope to encourage
churches that no longer have these events to reestablish
this warm tradition, and we urge churches that have never
experienced a homecoming to initiate such a celebration.

Traditional homecoming days follow a basic pattern:

> Regular Sunday morning services
> Dinner on the grounds (for you city folk, a picnic)
> Cleaning of the cemetery (if there is one)
> Singing and preaching
> Visiting and fellowship

This schedule can provide a warm and meaningful
event. Some churches may not want to deviate from it, and
that's okay! Others might like to try another approach on
occasion. Here are several suggestions that will add
variety to homecoming programs.

Although these ideas are aimed primarily at churches,
they could be used also for family and other types of
reunions.

An Old-fashioned Homecoming—Appoint committees
to serve in the areas of food, shelter, games, singing,
decoration, publicity, and services. Suggest that guests
wear old-fashioned clothing (long dresses, bonnets, and
shawls for the women; top hats, split-tail coats, beards for
the men). Some guests could arrive in horse-drawn
buggies or wagons, if available.

If a cemetery is not a part of the church grounds, construct one with fake tombstones or markers. A hitching post, an old church bell, a well (this prop to be used for tossing in coins for missions) could add to the atmosphere. A museum could contain antique items (churns, plows, candle holders, pictures, etc.).

Horseshoes, hopscotch, softball, volleyball, croquet, quilting bee, and spelling bee are just a few activities that could be included.

Dinner on the grounds is a picnic affair, with ice-cold lemonade supplied by the church or other host. A sing-a-long can be held outdoors or in the church. Special music by family groups, quartets, soloists, or instrumentalists can add to the festivities. A church event can conclude with a sermon by the pastor or by a former pastor.

Grand Ole Homecoming—A country-western flavor can enhance this get-together. Encourage everyone to wear this type clothing. Sell tickets for an old-fashioned barbeque with slaw, beans, corn bread, and iced tea served from a chuck wagon. The dessert can be ice cream and/or Brownies*. The guests can eat under shade trees or in large tents. Erect a split-rail fence, with posts holding a sign that reads CEDAR CREEK RANCH (with letters that appear to have been made with a branding iron).

A country-western museum can display programs, posters, photographs, and souvenirs from country-western events or fairs. Old-fashioned dress or present-day outfits can be displayed. Some hobby collections such as salt and pepper shakers, matchcovers, and such might enhance this museum.

Audition for your own country-western show by enlisting members to sing, play an instrument, or just clown around. Construct the front of a red barn for the stage area, or use a large sign: CEDAR CREEK OPRY. The microphone stand could be covered with a sign reading C. C. Opry. Have a master of ceremonies introduce each act. If there are people in the community who can perform, use them. Make your Opry full of fun and entertainment. Each segment of the program can be sponsored by a church organization or ministry: "This portion of the Cedar Creek Opry is brought to you by your Sunday school. Sunday school at Cedar Creek begins at 9:00 A.M. Come to Sunday school."

The last segment of your Opry can feature gospel quartets, soloists, or instrumentalists. Allow time for a closing message from the pastor or guest preacher.

All-American Homecoming—This idea incorporates a July Fourth celebration. Use a patriotic theme with decorations that depict Independence Day. Have a museum of historic memorabilia. Dress can be from colonial or any other period of American history. Dinner on the grounds could be the all-American hot dog or hamburger with trimmings.

The afternoon can feature softball or field-day events. An old-fashioned political debate could pit two make-believe candidates against each other. The topic of the debate should be humorous. "Should the community forbid fireflies to light up at night?" Then hold a mock election.

A brush arbor or a large tent can serve for a place to gather for services.

Present a summer music festival by your choir(s), combining good gospel songs with patriotic music. The theme of the pastor's homecoming message can be "Freedom."

A Homecoming Retreat or Campout—Publicize well in advance that the church is going on a weekend homecoming retreat or campout. Urge everyone to save that date for the church trip to a state park, a church camp, or a campground. Suggested schedule:

Saturday: 8:00 A.M.—Leave for retreat site
9:30 —Arrive, check-in
10:00 —Conference: A History of Our Church
11:30 —Break for lunch
2:00 P.M.—Softball or volleyball
3:30 —Swimming
5:00 —Free time
6:00 —Chow down
7:30 —Conference: A Look at the Coming Year
8:30 —Break (homemade desserts)
9:00 —Fellowship: games, singing, skits
10:30 —Off to bed

Sunday: 8:00 A.M.—Breakfast
9:30 —Bible study or church school
11:00 —Service by the lake
12:00 —Lunch
1:30 P.M.—Family Albums: Introduce each family present, tell when they joined the church, list offices held, etc.
2:30 —Sing-along
3:00 —Service by the lake
4:00 —Adjourn

Whatever you do for homecoming, do it well! Enjoy the planning, involve the people, use your imagination. Other Suggestions: Have an all-day sing; have a carnival; make a historical movie or slides of the church; have a crafts fair; present a pageant or religious drama.

Enjoy your homecoming!!

3

FUN WITH PARTIES

The trend toward informal types of recreation is a wholesome one. It allows for more spontaneity, emphasizes a variety of possible activities, and gives participants an opportunity to choose what they want to do. It releases the group from rigidity and makes it possible to follow the leads indicated by the moods and interests of the participants. Sensing the value of this informal and varied program, many groups have wisely swung to the open-house type of program with a wide variety of games and activities going on simultaneously, thus making it unnecessary to herd everyone into the same activity.

However, in our enthusiasm for this freer type of program, we must not lose sight of the values of the *theme party* as a useful agent in a well-rounded recreation program. A theme stimulates imagination, provides a basis for unity, suggests a decorative scheme that provides atmosphere, makes it possible to avoid monotonous sameness, and assists the guests in remembering the occasion. This latter is more valuable than may be apparent. A good recreational event should be enjoyed three times—in anticipation, in realization, and in retrospect. In addition to its value at the time of the activity, the theme party has anticipatory and retrospective values not common to the themeless recreation occasion.

Characteristics of a Good Party—Action, surprise, variety, spontaneity, balance (provided by "breathers" and the inclusion of a wide range of activities), smooth continuous movement, unity, climax, and an atmosphere of friendliness—these are some of the essentials to be kept in mind when planning party programs.

THE GREAT GRINMORE CIRCUS

Invitations or Publicity

STUPENDOUS*!* COLOSSAL*!* MAGNIFICENT*!*
THE GREATEST SHOW ON EARTH*!*
COME ONE*!* COME ALL*!*
Starts Promptly at 8:01 P.M.
SEE THE MAIN SHOW*!*
SEE THE GREATEST COLLECTION OF ODDITIES ON EARTH*!*
NO RAIN CHECKS ISSUED*!*

Program

The Barkers: A barker stands on a box or chair in front of each sideshow and begins spieling for his particular peformance. "Madame Utellum! Have your palm read!" "See the Teutonic Terror! He's plenty strong! Don't miss this great show!" "Hurry! Hurry! Hurry! There's a great show inside! Get in line, folks, get in line!"

Sideshows: Booths have been arranged. Posters advertise the mammoth exhibits. Large streamers speak convincingly of the wonders inside.

The possibilities in sideshows are limitless. Suggestions:

 The legless, hairless dog (a weiner)
 The Teutonic Terror (a bit of limburger)
 The wild baboon (a mirror)
 The only red bat in captivity (a brickbat tied with a string)

A trip around the world (Roll guest around globe map in wagon.)

Wild man from Borneo (painted and costumed man)

"For ladies only" (a hairpin)

"For men only" (suspenders)

Grand Stage Show: An announcer stands behind a screen and introduces each scene. If an amplifier can be provided, so much the better.

1. Clown Act
   a. Remains of Ancient Greece. The clown carries a candlestick which holds a burnt-out candle.
   b. Ruins of China. The clown drops broken china, gets a broom and sweeps it up.
   c. Our Own Native Land. Clown shows soil on garden spade.
   d. Yellowstone Park. The clown brings in a Park Here sign, then parks a yellow stone under the sign.

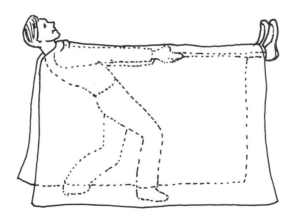

2. The Floating Man. A man lies (or appears to lie) on a table, covered with a sheet or blanket. What appear to be his feet are really just two shoes fitted onto the end of two poles or broomsticks. He stands behind the cover, holding

his head back. In his hands he holds the two poles with the shoes sticking out beyond the end of the cover. A magician makes a few mysterious passes over him and mutters the mystic words "Abba ka dabba." The man moves off, holding the sticks out in front of him. The sheet covers his body and gives the appearance of a man floating through the air. It might be well to tack the sheet to the poles so it will not slip, thus disclosing the man walking under it. Or this disclosure might be part of the fun.

3. The Dancing Midgets. Two or more of these midgets could be arranged by taking an old sheet and cutting holes for the head, legs, and arms. Pin tiny costumes on the outside of the sheet. The head of one person appears in the large hole in the sheet and this person's hands and arms (on which have been placed baby shoes and stockings) appear in the two holes cut for the midget's legs. A second person stands behind the first. The second person's arms are placed under the first person's armpits and through the arm holes, thus providing the midget's hands. A table is provided on which the midgets can dance. They may also talk, sing, or put on a skit. A bit of imagination will disclose the possibilities in this stunt.

side view

4. Puppet Show. A puppet or marionette show would be appropriate.

5. Mellerdrammer. A good take-off on melodrama would add to the fun of the evening. This plot, a little threadbare but still usable, might do in a pinch: The characters are Grandpa and Grandma; Little Nell, their pride and joy; the hero; and the villain, who holds a mortgage on the old homestead and threatens to foreclose unless he can have Little Nell. Naturally the hero appears in the nick of time to pay the mortgage and give the villain his just deserts.

The Circus Ring: The parade with the circus band and performers will announce the ring performance. There will be clowns, animals (and oh, what animals!), a strong man, a two-headed girl, some real tumblers, and whatever else goes with a circus performance.

Refreshments—Hot dogs, Chocolate-chip Oatmeal Cookies*, and pink lemonade, served by the clowns.

A FANTASYLAND PARTY

Invitations

> Put on kid's clothes,
> And goodness knows,
> Follow your nose
> To Fantasyland.
> There happiness grows,
> And joy supreme flows,
> So everyone goes
> To Fantasyland.

Program

The Sugar Plum Tree: In the first room the guests find the Sugar Plum Tree, a small bush on which hang sticks of candy. Each guest may take a stick.

The Nursery: Before entering Fantasyland, or The Enchanted Forest, the sticky hands must be clean. Therefore all guests must pass through the nursery where a nurse washes and wipes their hands. If the crowd is large only a gesture may be made.

Fantasyland: Decorate with vines, foliage, toy balloons, angel hair, animals peeping through the foliage. Achieve a blue lighting effect by covering all the lights with blue gelatin, cellophane, or crepe paper. Over in one corner have a wishing well. Hang numerous strings out over the sides of this well. At the end of each string is an answer to the wish of the one who pulls it.

A Scrambled Fairy Tale: Each of several people is given the title of a different fairy story. One person is designated to begin the story and another to finish it. Each tells a portion of the story at a time designated by the leader. No person is allowed more than thirty seconds. The sequences in this jumbled story promise lots of fun, as they skip from Little Red Riding Hood to the Little Red Hen to the Three Bears to Jack and the Bean Stalk, etc.

Fairy Tale Rebuses
1. ginleesptubaye
2. ylibltagoufgfr
3. thonewswi
4. seergthipteltil
5. ttielledriinrdgodho
6. lentiledhert
7. baterepbrit
8. eecalrdlni
9. hoipncoic
10. cogdilklos

Answers: (1) Sleeping Beauty (2) Billy Goat Gruff (3) Snow White (4) Three Little Pigs (5) Little Red Riding Hood (6) Little Red Hen (7) Peter Rabbit (8) Cinderella (9) Pinocchio (10) Goldilocks

Fairy Tale Dramatizations: This will probably prove the most enjoyable feature of the evening. Divide the crowd into three or four groups. Storytellers should be selected several days before the party and asked to be ready with designated stories and plans for their dramatization, including materials and ideas for costuming. These storytellers are assigned to the various groups to act as advisers, as well as storytellers, in helping the groups plan their stunts. Both the storyteller and the group may give their own interpretation to a story. Suggestions:

1. Red Riding Hood. One group had a lot of fun with this story. A young man wore a red hood, a red dress, and white pantaloons, achieved by pinning newspapers to his trousers. The wolf wore a dog falseface. The storyteller and the actors collaborated in bringing the story to the proper climax.

2. The Three Bears. Small tables, benches, chairs, and bowls furnish the necessary properties. The tables and benches become "beds." Goldilocks enters. She tries out the porridge and eats with relish the smallest portion. She tries the chairs and the "beds" and "goes to sleep" on the smallest. The bears arrive. Deep-crowned hats and fur-collared coats worn backward can serve as costumes. From then on the dramatization can move with rapid pace to the climax when Goldilocks escapes.

Children's Games: In Fantasyland it would be appropriate to play children's games—London Bridge, Sugar-Loaf Town, I Come to See Miss Jenny Ann Jones, Looby Loo, Farmer's in the Dell, Red Rover, Drop the Handkerchief, and Duck, Duck, Goose.

Refreshments—Cotton candy, popcorn, pink lemonade.

SCAVENGER HUNT PARTIES

Here are a number of ways to vary an old favorite. Add to, adapt, delete, recreate, or combine these ideas to suit your particular locale.

Old-fashioned Scavenger Hunt—Announce to the guests that everyone is to go on a scavenger hunt. Divide guests

into even groups of two to four and hand each group a
printed list of items to bring back. They are to go to homes
and try to gather the items. Suggestions:

1. Brown paper bag (for items you collect)
2. Piece of unused dental floss
3. Lemon
4. Magazine
5. Sock (clean)
6. Used bar of soap
7. Nail file
8. Empty (or almost) toothpaste tube
9. Toothpick
10. Needle and thread
11. Old shoe
12. Old hat
13. Nail
14. Empty can
15. Pencil

Alphabet Scavenger Hunt—Assign a letter of the
alphabet to each guest. The guest is to find as many items
as possible beginning with that letter. Example: The
person assigned the letter A could gather Apples. This
game could also be used for nature items; the guest
assigned the letter B might bring back a Bug or several
Bugs. When all have returned, they share their items and
tell the experiences they had.

Penny Scavenger Hunt—Give each person one penny.
Guests are to go to five homes. At the first home, they are to
exchange the penny for an item; at the second home, they
are to exchange the item for another item (hopefully of
more value). This process continues for five homes. Guests
return with the fifth item.

Variation: Give five pennies to each guest. A penny is to
be exchanged for an item at each of five homes. Guests are
to return with five items.

Nature Scavenger Hunt—If at a camp or near some woods, assign the individuals objects to bring back. Examples:

1. Large leaf
2. Small mushroom
3. Whitest rock
4. Funny stick
5. Snail or slug
6. Pine needle or small evergreen branch
7. Flowers
8. Moss
9. Bark from a tree
10. Pinecone or Sweetgum ball

Pocketbook Scavenger Hunt—If for an older group of men and women, have the group divide into teams. Each team should have equal numbers of women with purses and men with wallets. Call out each item and the first group to respond gets a point. Suggestions:

1. Set of keys
2. Lighter
3. Credit card
4. Photograph
5. Earring
6. Lipstick
7. Coughdrops or mints
8. Mirror
9. Flashlight
10. Hairpin

Miniature or Indoor Scavenger Hunt—Choose about 20 items for this scavenger hunt. Before the guests arrive, hide the items around the room or make them as inconspicuous as possible. Give each person a printed list and a pencil. On the signal, each person is to individually locate the items and write the locations in the space provided.

Item	*Location*
1. Straight pin	_____
2. Piece of masking tape	_____
3. Hairpin	_____
4. Bible	_____
5. Piece of red construction paper	_____
6. Thimble	_____
7. Piece of yarn	_____
8. Broom	_____
9. Paperclip	_____
10. Paper cup	_____
11. Pencil	_____
12. Newspaper	_____
13. A living plant	_____
14. Old rag	_____
15. Coin	_____

The first to complete the list is the winner.

Photo Scavenger Hunt—An instant camera and film for each team is needed for this hunt. Give each team a list of photographs to be taken and a camera already loaded with film. The first group to return with the correct photographs wins. Caution the drivers of the automobiles to drive within the speed limit and to be very careful. As many of the group as possible are to be in each photo. Suggestions:

1. Stand under a bank's electronic clock with a designated time showing on the clock. (25 points)

2. Stand with a clerk at a local hotel or motel. (15 points)

3. Shake hands with a policeman at his patrol car. (30 points)

4. Stand with a group of people in a bathtub. (5 points for each person in the tub)

5. Stand at a fountain, statue, or historical marker in the community. (15 points)

6. Go to the home of a teacher and pose with him or her. (15 points)

7. Pack a phone booth. (10 points for each person)

8. Change someone's tire. (50 points)

9. Go to a restaurant and pose with everyone who is willing. (5 points a person)

10. Pose with an animal. (10 points)

Mount each team's photographs on posterboard for display. Add up the points for the winning team.

Four-wheel Scavenger Hunt—Enlist safe drivers for this game. Give each car team a list of items to bring back. Suggestions:

1. A book of matches imprinted with the name of a hotel or motel.

2. A hamburger from a fast-food restaurant.

3. A shopping bag from a local department store.

4. A flower and a greeting card from a florist.

5. A charge slip stamped with the name of a service station.

6. The autograph of a schoolteacher.

7. A cone without the ice cream.

8. A trading stamp from a store.

9. A church bulletin.

10. A piece of fruit from a grocery store.

The first group back with the required items wins.

Refreshments—Party Cheese Ball*, chips and crackers, dips, cold beverages.

A PIONEER PARTY

Publicity—Advertise with a miniature covered wagon. A small basket, a bit of white crepe paper for the cover, and some heavy cardboard for wheels would do the trick. If guests will agree to come in costume it will add to the fun.

Decorations—If some pioneer relics can be borrowed—a spinning wheel, an old musket, a tripod and kettle—it will assist in creating the atmosphere desired.

Program

Pioneer Music: As guests arrive, gather around the piano to sing some of the old songs: "Oh, Susanna," "Camptown Races," "Old Folks at Home," "Juanita," "Silver Threads Among the Gold," "Love's Old Sweet Song," "The Old Chisholm Trail," "Sweet Alice Ben Bolt," "My Old Kentucky Home," "In the Evening by the Moonlight."

Pioneer Games: Use some of the old musical games: Jennie Cracks Corn, The Old Brass Wagon, Bingo, Brown-eyed Mary, Oh, Susanna, Looby Loo, Virginia Reel.

Pioneer Charades: Work out charades on such words as *pioneer* (pie-on-ear or pie-oh-near), *Standish* (stand-dish), *Davy Crockett* (day-vie-crock-eat), *Daniel Boone* (Dan-yell-boon), *Samuel Houston* (Sam-you-well-hue-stone).

Pioneer Drama:

PRECIOUS PRISCILLA

CAST

PRECIOUS PRISCILLA, the pretty princess (She flutters to the center of the stage, curtsies, bows, and exits.)

PIOUS PAUL, a peppy pal (He is dressed in gypsy costume, comes in taking long steps, tips his hat several times to the audience, and exits.)

PETRIFIED PETE, the Pawnee papa (He comes on the stage stealthily and scowls at the crowd.)

PREVARICATIN' PAT, the Pawnee's partner (He follows just a few steps behind Pete and imitates him exactly.)

PEGGY PERUNY, the poisonous prattler (She is indifferent to everybody.)

PRIMITIVE POLLY, the plucky pet of the plains (She is snappy, comes in with hands on hips. She may be a gypsy.)

All italicized parts are read by someone and the characters act out their parts. After all the characters have been introduced, the reader begins the story, being careful to read clearly and distinctly so the audience will have no trouble understanding.

Precious Priscilla, the pretty princess, parts from the palace for the prosperous plains. (She walks across the stage backward, throwing kisses toward the wings, and runs into Pious Paul, who has been watching her with interest. She shows surprise. He suggests a walk, offers his arm, and they leave in the direction Priscilla was going.)

Primitive Polly peers 'pon her pal and Precious Priscilla. Her poor pulse palpitates painfully. (Polly enters, registers jealousy.)

Petrified Pete and Prevaricatin' Pat plot to pounce 'pon Precious Priscilla and plunder the plains. (Pete and Pat tiptoe stiffly to center stage, plot together, scan the horizon. They go to opposite corners of the stage, then come back to center.)

They park behind a pile of pebbles. (They take two or three steps and squat.)

Precious Priscilla plods the plains plucking posies. (She zigzags over the stage, very elaborately breaking off flowers, occasionally smelling the bunch. She even picks some off Pete's head, ignoring the fact that he is there.)

She sits on prickly pear. (You know the action.)

She perches 'pon peanut near pebbles. (She assumes sitting posture beside Pete and Pat.)

Pete and Pat pounce 'pon her. (They creep up on either side and grab her. Priscilla registers screaming. They gag her and swing her back and forth as though wrestling.)

They put her 'pon pony and part from plains. (The three step back, take high steps as though mounting, and gallop off, Pete pulling reins, Priscilla screaming, Pat slapping an imaginary horse. They may use broomsticks or just imagine they are on horses. Height contrast is wanted here.)

Primitive Polly pears 'pon them and promptly protects Priscilla by persuading Paul to pursue. (Enter Paul on horseback. He stops and acts dismounting, listens to Polly, motions her up behind. They gallop off.)

Pete and Pat progress. (They gallop across stage left to right, going in circles.)

Paul's prancing pony is pricked by pointed posies and grows punk. (Both hop heavily on one foot, dragging other.)

Pete procures paddlewagon and proceeds. (They paddle slowly.)

Paul and Polly procure another paddlewagon and resume pursuit. (Paul in front takes long dignified strokes, Polly behind takes short, wild dashes as they approach center stage.)

Paul's paddlewagon hits pesky protruding prong. (Polly goes over the side. Three short strokes, one long one, Polly climbs back in, then all is as calm as before.)

Peruny is perched 'pon pallet, perplexed at Pete's not producing plunder. (She comes in and squats at back center.)

Pete pitilessly pitches Precious Priscilla 'pon pallet. Produces poison and plans to poison her. (Have large bottle labeled poison with water inside. They try to make her drink the poison.)

Paul and Polly prevent poisoning by pitching pepper at Pawnee. (Much sneezing and Pawnee falls over dead.)

Primitive Polly, having played her part, plunges penknife into her penetrable part and pays the penalty. (While the lovers embrace, Polly in center stage takes knife and with great deliberation stabs herself. She first tries to make it go in her head, then stabs her heart and falls over backward. Paul goes to her side, feels her pulse, sees she is dead. Returns to Priscilla. They look regretfully at Polly. Paul takes off his hat, Priscilla wipes a tear.)

Curtain.

—ELIZABETH FORREST FARRIS

Refreshments—Cheesy Walnut Pinwheels*, Sour Cream Pie*, coffee or hot chocolate.

A YEAR 2025 PARTY

Invitations

Now use your imagination,
And out of your cogitation
Figure what will happen in 2025 A.D.
Dress twenty-first century style;
Have a big time for awhile;
A grand good party you can bet it will be.

Decorations—Futuristic pictures and other decorations. Guests may come in clothing that might be worn in the year 2025.

Program

Passing Fancies: Each guest is given paper and pencil and asked to name a thing which will be only a memory in A.D. 2025. These are shuffled and passed out. Each guest must then read the passing fancy and suggest some substitute for it. Suggestions: rock music, the art of conversation, lipstick, men's ties, battleships, college athletics, newspapers.

Desired Inventions: Have guests suggest the most useful invention or discovery by the year 2025.

Fashions: Give each couple bits of cheesecloth, scraps of material, ribbons, old hat frames, plenty of newspapers, pins, tape, and anything else available. Have each man dress his partner in the sort of costume he thinks women will wear in A.D. 2025. In a very large crowd, the designs could be achieved by groups, each group selecting one person to dress.

Rhythm Design: Have each person experiment with rhythm design. Pans of water are made available. Someone starts to swirl the water gently until it is moving in circular fashion. Then a drop or two of India ink (or any ink that is oily) is dropped into the swirling water. Now white sheets of paper are dipped into the pan. All sorts of fascinating patterns appear. Care should be taken not to smear the ink either in removing the paper or after taking the design out of the water. Allow the paper to dry and then have guests develop designs from the patterns. Some exceedingly interesting designs will be created. It may be necessary to go on with some of the rest of the program while the papers dry, allowing the artists to finish their creations later in the evening.

The March of Time: Divide into groups and give each group two minutes to dramatize some typical daily happening the year A.D. 2025.

Futuristic Art: Give each person a card, some confetti, and a dab of paste. Allow three minutes for the creation of some futuristic design to be achieved by sprinkling the confetti on the wet paste. Label the picture and put them on display. Suggestions for titles: "Sunset on the Beach," "A Storm," "Thoughts of You," "An Evening in Space."

Looking Backward: It would be appropriate for someone to give an interesting and brief description or skit of a person of the nineteenth century awakening in the year 2025.

Refreshments—Sandwiches, cookies, and chocolate milk.

A PROGRESSIVE ATHLETIC CARNIVAL

This party could take place either indoors or outdoors. Divide the crowd into small groups of equal numbers—say four, six, or eight to a group. Most of the games can be table games. Have table and play spaces arranged and numbered so it will be easy for the players to progress in order. Numbers and directions can be printed on cards and placed in standards on the tables.

All players at a game progress to the next game when the leader blows a whistle. Thus during the evening, each person will play in each game. Even though a group has finished a game, it does not progress until the leader signals for progression. Otherwise, confusion would reign.

Scores are kept in each game and noted by each player on a tally sheet. After each group has made the rounds, total high and low scores are announced. Thus the evening's Champion and Champ-nit are discovered. Awards may be made to these two.

Select games that will require about the same length of time. Suggestions:

Basketball: Bounce tennis ball into a wastebasket at a distance of about ten feet. Point for each ball going into basket on first bounce. Five throws make a turn.

Bowling: Use five long-necked bottles and a baseball. Three throws for a turn. Limit game to two rounds.

Markmanship: Make target of soft wood (corrugated board). Outer circle counts 1, next circle 2, then 3, 4, and 5 in the center. Use regulation darts. Players cast darts at distance of ten to fifteen feet. Three throws for a turn.

Quoits: Drive a long nail into a piece of wood about three inches square. The nail serves as a peg. Use jar rings for quoits. Two to five throws. Ringer counts three; touching peg counts two, touching the wooden base counts one.

Baseball: Use a soft wood board about two feet long and a good knife with two blades at one end. The smaller blade is opened all the way; the other blade only half-way. Player touches this latter blade lightly to the board, with forefinger under end of knife handle, then flips knife over. If the small blade enters the board, thus causing the knife to stick straight up with no other part of it touching the board, a home run is made and the player scores four points. If the small blade sticks in the board, but the other blade touches the wood, it is a three-bagger, and three points are scored. If the large blade supports the knife alone, a two-bagger and two points. If the large blade and handle touch the board, a single and one point. If the knife lands on its back and stands up in that position, no play, and the player tries again. If the knife falls over, no score.

Marble Shooting: Make three holes at the bottom edge of a piece of heavy cardboard or a straight piece of board. Center hole should be about one inch in diameter and the two side holes about one and one-half inches. Center hole counts five. Others count one. Players shoot marbles as in regular game, or they may roll the marbles. Three shots count a turn. Any player getting two holes in succession gets extra shot.

Jacks: Use set of jacks and small rubber ball. Play as in regular game.

Tennis Rules: Each player is provided with paper and pencil and is to make as many words as possible out of the letters in "tennis rules," working until the whistle blows. No letter can be used in a word more often than it appears in the two words given. Suggestions: ten, net, leer, lure, utensil. One point for each word. Have a dictionary handy.

Football: Cover a table with smooth wrapping paper and mark off a football field. Make football of empty eggshell. (By punching small holes in both ends of an egg and blowing into one hole, you can force the contents out the other end.) Paint to look like football. Each player takes a turn at blowing the "football" from the goal line at one end of the field. The space into which the football is blown indicates the score. If the egg goes outside the field the count is made from the point at which it went out. A player who blows the football all the way across the field scores ten points.

Refreshments—Lime Punch*, Banana-split Cake*.

A NAUTICAL PARTY

Decorations—One group reports on their party: We used the gymnasium which had a balcony running all around it. We placed tire "life preservers" around the balcony against the railing; and below the life preservers, at intervals around the balcony, were placed portholes of round gray disks of cardboard. The centers of the disks were cut out, leaving just enough to form a hinge so that the window could swing out. Blue tissuepaper was pasted over the hole. A canopy of blue and white crepe-paper streamers was placed over the entire room, with a moon in one corner.

At the nearest naval recruiting station we were able to secure a number of large posters and pictures of ships. These were placed on the walls around the room. The lights were covered with dark blue tissuepaper, and large ropes were coiled and hung around the room. In the doorway was a gangplank made of two planks. Blocks were placed under one end, and upright pieces on the sides were connected with ropes.

Program—For 125 to 150 people, though a smaller crowd may also enjoy it. Instead of using a whistle for a signal, secure someone who can play the cornet or bugle and use some simple military calls. The bugle can sound Assembly for the "chaplain" to give the invocation.

Guests are given a word of welcome to the ship for the evening's cruise. The anchor is weighed by drawing it up to a balcony, if there is one available. If not, it can be placed on scales in the middle of the floor and actually weighed. The anchor can be made from black cardboard.

Mixer: A Recruiting Game. Copies of an enlistment form can be given out (p. 67), and at a signal, each guest begins to recruit for the navy. The one having the most names at the end of the period receives a prize (toy airplane or boat).

Crew Regatta: Each guest has been given a program with the name of one of the following ships: Monitor, Merrimac, Old Ironsides, Pinta, Maria, Mayflower, Maine, Columbia. Life preservers are made by wrapping old tires with white crepe paper. These are placed at regular intervals around the room with the name of a ship on each. At the Regatta, guests gather at the life preserver of the ship indicated on their programs. When all crews have gathered, instruct them to elect captains. The Regatta will consist of a series of games in which the winning crews will receive prizes. Do not announce all the games, so that the program may be changed or shortened if necessary. Suggested games:

1. Walk the Plank. Have each crew send one person to center of the room. A number of chairs are placed in various places on the floor. The contestants are then blindfolded and lined up. At a given signal they are told to

NAVY RECRUITING FORM

Name	Address	Age	Weight	Health	Disposition	I.Q.	Married?
1.							
2.							
3.							
4.							
5.							
6.							
7.							
8.							
9.							
10.							
11.							
12.							
13.							
14.							
15.							
16.							
17.							
18.							
19.							
20.							
21.							
22.							
23.							
24.							
25.							

run as fast as possible to the other side of the room. Before they start, however, all or most of the chairs are noiselessly removed. First, second, and third places are recorded.

2. Fish Stories. Have each crew select one member to tell a fish story. They are called on one at a time, given two minutes to tell a story, and judges award first, second, and third places.

3. A Rush for the Boat. This is a relay. Line up each crew in single file with all the leaders on an even line. Place a chair at the other end of the room for each line of runners. Now place in front of each line a suitcase or handbag (preferably old ones). At a given signal (bugle blast) the leaders pick up the bags and run to the other end of the room, circle the chairs, and come back to their lines. The crew that finishes first, of course, wins. There should be the same number of players in each line.

4. Ships and Other Ships. This is a writing game. Each captain is given paper and pencil. At the signal of the bugle each crew is to think of (and their captain is to write down) words in which the word *ship* occurs: friendship, courtship, etc. At the end of two minutes, the papers are collected, the words counted, and first, second, and third places recorded.

Presentation of Grand Prize: A box of sea-foam candy or salt-water taffy.

Vessel Vespers: Use some of the old gospel hymns with a nautical theme: "Let the Lower Lights Be Burning," "Throw out the Lifeline."

Refreshments—Doughnuts covered with powdered sugar, and hot chocolate with floating marshmallows. Use carts decorated with crepe paper to represent ships. Girls and/or boys dressed in nautical-type clothing can serve. Provide music. If a whistle with the sound of a boat can be obtained, it can be blown just as the decorated carts enter the room.

A SHIP PARTY

This party should be held in a building where there is one room large enough to accommodate the entire group, in addition to several smaller rooms or available spaces: gyms, Sunday school buildings, community buildings, schoolhouses, civic centers.

Decorations—Anything nautical: life preservers, deck signs, paper pennants, etc. It could be a costume party, with guests dressed as sailors. However, passengers in a variety of costumes would lend atmosphere.

Make signs reading: B-Deck, Promenade Deck, Look Out for Sharks, Throw Things off Lee Side Only, Swimming Off Port Side—4:00–6:00 P.M., Ping-pong Tournament in Session, Ship News Out! etc. Place these signs where all can see them.

Cut tricornered pennants from colored paper (except crepe). Make enough for several strings across the ceiling. In other words, decorate as a ship for the gala last night out. Make "passports" from scraps left from cutting pennants.

Program—Each smaller room is to be named: Ballroom, Recreation Room, Lobby, Dining Salon, Pilot Room, Roost, Clubroom, Promenade Deck, Crow's Nest, etc. In each room, certain activities or games will take place, and passengers will rotate from room to room in groups.

Suggested activities: pencil games, fortunetelling, marble games, dart baseball, charades, table games (checkers, anagrams, etc.).

A food game is good for the dining salon. Set out several condiments such as cloves, pepper, vinegar, anything edible with a distinctive odor. Blindfold passengers and let each smell the articles and try to guess what each is.

The passengers are divided into groups according to size of group and number of games planned. Each passenger could be given a passport to some country—for instance, a certain number could receive green passports (Germany), and a certain number yellow ones (France), etc. In the large room, have large signs corresponding in color and country, on the wall. After the first get-together game or song, each passenger will go to his or her "country," and the rotation will start.

Passengers will be conducted by guides who have been previously instructed as to the order of rotation. At the sound of the ship's gong, groups will change rooms. Length of time at each game will be determined by number of groups and time allotted for entire party. There will, of course, be one of the crew in each of the game rooms to direct play.

At a special signal on the gong, all passengers will assemble in the largest room for the grand finale. This might be folk games, folksongs, or planned entertainment by the ship's crew.

Refreshments—Graham-cracker Cake* and punch.

DAYS OF YORE PARTY

Publicity—Include the fact that guests should bring photographs of themselves as babies or small children. Be sure to remind them to write their names on the back of the photographs. As guests arrive, collect the photographs for a game later on.

Program

Mixer: Hand each guest a pencil and a paper with the following questionnaire.

1. Name _____

2. Born: month ____ day ____ year ____ (optional)

3. Hometown _____

4. Life's vocation _____

5. Hobby _____

6. Number of children _____

7. Number of grandchildren _____

8. Number of great-grandchildren _____

Take up the papers and when the baby pictures are shown later, read the questionnaires.

Charades: A game played in days of yore was charades— a form of pantomime. Almost everyone enjoys acting, so let those who want to perform do so while all guess; or divide into groups to see which group can guess the answers first.

There are certain signs that will help the group guess the pantomime. Remember, the person performing cannot speak. These signs help show whether the charade is a book title, movie, or record:

Book. Hold hands together in front, opened like a book.

Movie. Hold left hand up to right eye as if looking through a telescope; with right hand pretend to turn crank.

Record. Hold left hand in front, palm up; point index finger of right hand toward left palm and move hand in a circle like the arm of a record player.

Suggestions for charades:

1. Books, Songs, Movies. Print on cards the names of books, songs, or movies of yesteryear. Be sure to tell the guests that these titles are from days of yore.

Books
Robinson Crusoe
Arrowsmith
Main Street

Songs
  "April Showers"
  "Toot, Toot, Tootsie!"
  "Swanee"
  "Sonny Boy"
  "Over There"
  "Bicycle Built for Two"
  "In the Evening by the Moonlight"
  "Carolina Moon"

Movies
  The Jazz Singer
  The Wizard of Oz
  The Great Dictator
  The Great Train Robbery
  Father of the Bride
  Meet Me in St. Louis
  State Fair
  Tarzan the Ape Man
  Heidi

2. Group Charades. Divide into several groups. Let each group choose someone to do the pantomime. Each pantomimist comes to the middle of the room and receives either a book title, song title, or movie title, and on the signal, begins to pantomime. The first group to guess gets points for its team. Use same titles as above.

3. Paper-bag Skits. Each group is given a paper bag with various articles in it. The groups then work up skits, and the other groups try to guess what they are trying to convey. The bag can contain any kind of item: hat, gloves, neckties, potato, pencil, peanut, or whatever.

Other Games

1. Thimble Pass. Seat the guests in a circle. The leader appoints someone to be IT. As a thimble is passed around the circle, IT tries to discover who has the thimble. Each person in the circle pretends to be passing the thimble. As

soon as IT discovers who has the thimble, they exchange places.

2. Gossip. With guests in a circle, the leader whispers a brief story in the ear of the person on the right. Say it only once. That person relates the story to the next person, and so on, until the story has gone around the circle. The last person tells the story out loud to the group. The leader then tells the original story. Here is a sample story:

"A man was shaving and accidently cut off his nose. As he grabbed for his nose, he dropped his razor, cutting off his toe. At the hospital they sewed his toe where his nose was, and his nose where his toe was, and when he sneezed he blew off his shoe."

3. Guess Who? While the other games are going on, have someone mount the guests' baby pictures on a piece of poster board or lay them out on a table. Place a number by each photograph—1, 2, 3, etc. Give each guest a pencil and a paper with numbers corresponding to those on the photographs. Let the guests try to guess whose photo each is.

Identify each photograph and read the biographical information of that person taken earlier. If a projector can be secured, show the photographs on a screen.

Devotional—Center your thoughts around the pleasant memories of past days. Lead the group to see that we should always look at each day as time to live for Christ. Our past should be meaningful, yet it should point toward opportunities as we grow stronger daily in the service of the Lord. Read from Philippians 1:19-26.

Refreshments—Boiled custard with whipped cream; Cold Cranberry Punch* and coffee.

Adapted from Bob and Carolyn Sessoms, *52 Complete Recreation Programs for Senior Adults* (Nashville: Convention Press, 1979), pp. 50-52. Used by permission.

A RODEO PARTY

Announce that guests are to come in costume, representing cowboys and Indians. Boots may or may not be worn. Sombreros are in style for headgear. A blanket and headpiece would answer for the Indians.

As guests arrive, tag them with names that are to be worn the rest of the evening. There could be Deadwood Dick, Sitting Bull, Deer Heart, Nell, Flo, and others equally colorful. The guests are to be called by these names throughout the evening. There should be a penalty for using correct names.

Pony Express: Form two concentric circles with the girls in the inner circle. As the music plays, boys march in one direction and girls in the other. When the leader blows a whistle each girl grabs a boy for a partner, turns, marches in the same direction the boys are going. All extra girls go to the center of the circle and wait there until the whistle blows again. This time the girls again reverse their direction and march as at first. This process continues until the leader feels the crowd has been fairly mixed. The music continues throughout. The boys do not stop or slow up when the whistle blows, but continue marching in the same direction. As soon as the whistle blows, each girl should immediately reverse her direction, keeping perfect time to the music.

Roundup: Two leaders are appointed. The crowd endeavors to keep out of their way. The leaders begin by tagging one player each, who then join hands with the leaders who tagged them. Each pair now endeavors to tag two others. As fast as players are tagged, they join hands with the group doing the tagging. Only end players can tag. Players tagged while the line is broken are free. If a line can encircle one or more players completely, they are considered tagged. Each leader endeavors to round up the larger number of players. When the game is played indoors, players are exempt from being tagged when they are touching a wall, but players may not claim this exemption for longer than ten seconds at a time.

Lariat Race: Ten players are selected to represent each side. They stand in single file. The first player is provided with a rope six feet or more in length. At the signal, the player must jump this rope, passing it over the head in doing so. The next player in line takes the rope and does the same thing. So it goes to the end of the line. The end player must then skip the rope to the head of the line and start it down again. When the first player is again at the head of the line, that team has finished the race.

Roping Contest: Divide into two teams. A lasso is provided for each team. These can be made by tying a noose in the end of a long rope. Players are given an opportunity to test their skill at lassoing the leg of an upturned chair. For each successful effort a point is awarded that team.

Stagecoach: Players stand or sit in a circle and number off by sevens. All 1s become cowboys; all 2s, Indians; all 3s, women; all 4s, horses; all 5s, stagecoaches; all 6s, rifles; and all 7s, bows and arrows. The leader then reads a story about the hold-up of a stage by Indians. When "cowboys" are mentioned, they pretend to be driving a stage at a furious pace and shout, "Yip! Yip!" The "Indians" war dance and yell. The "women" scream. The "horses" beat a tattoo on the floor with their feet or on their knees with their hands. The "stagecoachs" turn completely around. The "rifles" take aim and shout "Bang!" The "bows and arrows" drop to one knee or stand, draw the bow and shout "Zip!" Suggested story:

—It was in the days of *stagecoaches* and *cowboys* and *Indians.* Alkali Ike, Dippy Dick, and Pony Pete were three courageous *cowboys.* When the *stagecoach* left for Rainbow's End they were aboard, as were two *women,* Salty Sal

and Frosty Flo. The *stagecoach* was drawn by three
handsome *horses,* and it left Dead End exactly on time.

The most dangerous part of the journey was the pass
known as Gory Gulch. As the *stagecoach* neared this spot,
the *women* were a bit nervous and the *cowboys* were alert,
fingering their *rifles* as if ready for any emergency. Even
the *horses* seemed to sense danger.

Sure enough, just as the *stagecoach* entered the Gulch,
there sounded the blood-curdling war whoop of the *Indians.*
Mounted on *horses,* they came riding wildly toward the
stagecoach, aiming their *bows and arrows.* The *cowboys*
took aim with their *rifles* and fired. The *women* screamed.
The *horses* pranced nervously. The *Indians* shot their *bows
and arrows.* The *cowboys* fired their *rifles* again, this time
with more deadly effect. The leading brave fell, and the
Indians turned their *horses* and fled, leaving their *bows
and arrows* behind. The *women* fainted. The *cowboys* shot
once more with their *rifles,* just for luck. The driver urged
the *horses* on, and the *stagecoach* sped down the trail.

After the crowd has been divided into the seven groups,
it would be well to practice once before proceeding with the
story.

Indian Warbonnet Race: From four to ten players may
represent each side. The teams line up in shuttle-relay
style, with half of each team at one end of the room and half
at the other. The first player on each team wears an Indian
warbonnet. This may be made of chicken or turkey
feathers, if colored feathers are not available. At the
signal, this player hops to the opposite side of the room,
doffs the headgear, and hands it to teammate Number
Two. This teammate dons the warbonnet and hops across
to the next player on the other side of the room. So the
game continues until each player has been over the course.

Stagecoach Race: Form two teams. Two wheelbarrows
are provided. One person from each team pushes, while a
teammate rides. When they get to the opposite side of the
room, of course, they exchange places, and the former rider

guides the "stagecoach" back to the starting point. The first team in wins.

Bucking Contest: Divide players into two equal teams, then form one big circle. In the center of the circle, place a saddle or sofa pillow. At the signal, each side begins pulling, endeavoring to make some player on the opposing side touch the saddle. To avoid it, a player may jump. Any player who touches the saddle must drop out of the circle. At the end of five minutes of strenuous pulling and bucking, the team with the most players still in the game is declared the winner.

Refreshments—Barbecue sandwiches, coffee, and ice-cream cones.

A CAMERA PARTY

Invitations

Look pleasant, please, and come around,
For a camera party has hit this town.

This party might follow a camera hike or hunt. The pictures should be mounted and put on display, or slides could be made so the pictures can be shown on a screen.

Program

Baby Pictures: Gather baby pictures of many of those who are to attend, number them, and put them on display. Guests are given paper and pencils and asked to guess "Who's Who." After a given time, announce the correct list. Players check their own lists.

Spirit Pictures: Guests are taken into a dark room where they are told some spirit pictures are to be taken. In one corner of the room a light is flashed, showing a ghost. The light plays on the figure for just a moment and is then turned off. Again it flashes and a skeleton is seen standing

there. The third time it flashes the head of a young girl
appears, apparently severed from the body and pinned to a
white sheet by the hair. Beneath her head are splotches of
what seems to be blood.

The skeleton and ghost should appear before a black
background. The former is made by sewing white cloth, cut
to represent a skeleton, to the black cloth.

The girl's head is stuck through a slit in a sheet. Her face
is whitened to give it a ghastly appearance. The hair is
drawn up and pinned to the sheet. Red ink is daubed below
the slit.

Spoon Photography: Two confederates are needed for
this stunt. One goes out of the room. The other one remains
and with a silver spoon, professes to take the picture of
some player simply by holding the spoon in front of that
player's face. The player who went out of the room is called
back and, when looking intently into the spoon, tells what
player's picture was taken. (The photographer is always to
take the picture of the person who speaks last before the
confederate leaves the room. Or it may be the person to the
right of the talker, or some other signal that will easily
designate the proper person.)

Retouching: Each person is provided with a paper spoon.
On tables are crayons or colored pens, pencils, crepe paper,
and paste. Players make Kamera Kuties, using red crayon
or paint for the cheeks and lips, the pencil to mark the
features, and crepe paper for the dress. These Kuties may
be used as souvenirs of the occasion.

Load the Camera: Divide the crowd into two groups.
Have each side represented by three players. The first runs
to a designated point, deposits a camera, returns, and
touches the next player. That player runs to the same
point, carrying a roll of film, returns, and touches the third
player, who rushes forward, loads the camera, and returns
to the starting point with it.

"Smile, Please": Three to six players represent each side. They line up facing the crowd. While the leader counts ten slowly, all players must hold a smiling expression. Immediately when "ten" is reached, the smiles must fade out and serious expressions take their place. These too are held until ten is counted. This is continued for three full turns. Whenever players fail to immediately change expression and hold it, they must drop out. The crowd may do its best to make players laugh when they ought to appear glum. At the end of the three rounds the side with the largest number of players left standing is declared winner. When no players are left standing, champions for each side may be selected to fight it out.

Focus: Make a beanbag board with a hole just big enough for the beanbag to go through. Line up both sides and allow each player one throw. One point is scored each time the beanbag goes through the hole. If desired, a board with three to five holes in it may be used, in which case the player gets as many throws as there are holes. It may be required that the beanbag must go through a different hole each time. Time will be saved by having beanbags for each side.

Mounting: Line up five to ten players for each side. A small matchbox top is provided each side. The first player fits the matchbox on his or her nose. At the signal, the player must transfer it to the nose of the next player without using hands. Thus it goes from nose to nose until the end of the line is reached. If the box falls, the player whose turn it is must pick it up and resume the race.

Framing: Make a ring-toss board that can be hung on the wall. A board twelve by eighteen inches will do. Insert five small screw-hooks. Some jar rings complete your equipment. The center hook counts ten points. The four corner hooks count five points each.

Players stand at a distance of six feet and try to land the rings on the hooks. Each contestant gets five tries. In a large crowd, just one.

Silhouettes: Stretch a sheet across a platform. Form two teams. Select players from each team to do some shadow posing behind the sheet. Judges should decide which team offers the best pictures. Short movies or shadow pictures may be offered instead of still pictures. Leaders may be appointed before the night of the party to work up suitable shadow-picture stunts. Costumes and paraphernalia that may be useful to the performers should be at their disposal. All lights should be turned off except the one back of the curtain. Performers stand between the light and the curtain.

Developing: Players are furnished with paper and pencil. Each player draws a short line—curved, straight, crooked, or wiggly, then passes the paper to the player on the right. This player must use the line to draw something. It might be advisable to label each finished creation so others will be able to tell what it is.

"The Photographer": Scene: A photographer's studio. Characters: photographer, farmer, old maid, flapper, jelly-bean, newlyweds, take-off on pastor or other notable. Properties: A tripod, small box, large black cloth, toy balloon, pin.

Various characters enter, pose for pictures. The last person should represent some prominent member of the group. When the photographer attempts to take this picture there is an explosion, the tripod is upset, and confusion reigns. The photographer shouts "You've broken my camera!" Curtain.

The explosion may be achieved by bursting a toy balloon under the cloth covering the "camera," or a paper sack may be burst offstage.

Refreshments—Coconut Cake* and Wedding Reception Punch*.

A PHOTO PARTY

Baby Pictures—You Yesteryear: Have each guest bring a baby picture to be placed on display. Number each picture (also write down the owner's name so you can remember). Give guests pencil and paper. Let them attempt to guess to whom the pictures belong and write the names at the appropriate numbers on the paper. Let guests check their own papers as you call out the correct answers.

A Current Shot—You Today: As guests arrive, take a polaroid shot of each person. When the Baby Pictures game is completed, add the current shot next to each person's baby picture.

Video Scavenger Hunt: Follow directions for the Photo Scavenger Hunt, using an instant camera or video tape camera to capture the event. After the scavenger hunt, display the photographs or show the video tape on the TV.

Refreshments—Banana Bread*, with coffee, tea, milk, or a special punch.

THE NAME'S THE GAME

Guess a Nickname: Give a 3 X 5 card and a pencil to each person. Guests should sign their given names and nicknames on the cards. The cards should then be placed in a box.

Then hand each guest a 4 X 5 card like the one illustrated on the following page.

Guests are to have each blank autographed with the given names of other players (not nicknames), until all blanks are filled. When the card is full, the player may sit down.

H	O	W	D	Y

The leader draws a card from the box, calls out the nickname written on the card, and everyone guesses who that person is. Upon identification of the player whose name is called, the other players put an X in the space on the card where that player signed it. THEN—the identified player must tell the meaning of the nickname, and how he or she received it.

Do this with all the cards until everyone has been introduced. However, the first player who crosses out *every name* on the card shouts "Howdy!" and is the winner of a small inexpensive prize.

What's My Name? Ahead of time, prepare cards with the names of famous people. Have the group stand in a circle, and with masking tape, place the cards on the backs of the players. After choosing a partner, players are to ask each other questions that can be answered yes or no, to find out who they are supposed to be. Example: The name of George Washington may be taped on a person's back. That player might ask, "Am I dead?" The answer is yes! Then, "Am I a political figure?" The answer would be yes! This goes on until the person guesses correctly. Hints may be given to help those who seem a little slow. When both partners have identified themselves, they sit down.

Acrostic Name: Give each guest another piece of paper or blank card, or use the back of the HOWDY card. Guests are to write their last name down the page, and beside each letter, write a word describing themselves. Example:

> F   - friendly
> L   - likes jelly beans
> O   - occupational choice: teacher
> Y   - yellow is favorite color
> D   - dresses preppy

Refreshments—Provide small cakes or cupcakes, icing mix, and different-flavored sprinkles. Let each person autograph or decorate a cake. Ice cream with a choice of toppings would add to this idea.

AN INDOOR BEACH PARTY

Publicity—Posters may be used to advertise the party. One could bear the slogan: Get in the Swim at the Indoor Beach Party. Another might play up this jingle:

> "Mother dear, may I go to swim?"
> "Yes, my darling daughter;
> Attend the Indoor Beach Party,
> And don't go near the water."

Appropriate pictures could be clipped from magazines to adorn these posters.

Decorations—These may be elaborate or not, as time, money, ingenuity, and good sense direct. The imagination of the guests will supply many details. There should be two or more beaches, depending on the size of the crowd. Say there are four—Atlantic City, Palm Beach, Ocean Grove, and Waikiki. (Names of local beaches may be substituted.)

Atlantic City would occupy one corner of the room. When we think of Atlantic City, we think of the "boardwalk." By a stretch of the imagination, suggest this beach by improvising a boardwalk in front of it. Bright-colored bathing suits could adorn the wall. Palm Beach is easy if a couple of palms could be borrowed. In a pinch, palm-leaf fans could be used. Imitation oranges could be made of crepe paper and tied to twigs adorned with artificial leaves. The Ocean Grove corner could have a background of shrubbery. Heavily leaved branches of trees matted against the wall might give the desired effect. Or if a dark blue curtain drop of some sort could be secured for a background, a white paper sailboat could be pinned on the sea of blue. Waikiki Beach could be represented by a drawing of Diamond Head, with surfboards, flowers, and colorful sailboats.

It might be best to appoint a leader for each beach before the night of the party. As guests arrive they are assigned to one of the groups. Different sorts of contests are now introduced. Each group, of course, should have its own cheers and songs.

Program

Boardwalk Race: Three people from each group. Two walk or run, as decided, the length of the room and back, carrying the third between them on a piece of board about thirty inches long. Award points for first, second, and third places.

Swimming Race: One person represents each beach. Each contestant has a deep piepan filled nearly to the brim with water. At the bottom of the pan rest four or five lifesavers. These must be gotten out with the mouth. The hands must be clasped behind the back.

High Dive: One person from each beach. Each is provided with a pitcher of water. On the floor is an empty tumbler. This must be filled at least two-thirds full from standing position. Accuracy, not speed, is the test here. The one who spills the least water on the floor is declared winner. Should there be a tie in the minds of the judges, then the matter of time consumed may be taken into account.

Life-saving Feat: Two people from each beach. One stands at a distance of five paces from the other and is supplied with ten lifesavers. These are tossed one at a time to the other person, who endeavors to catch them with the mouth. The partners who are most successful win for their group.

Clam Dig: One person from each beach. A box of sand will be necessary. Hide ten peanuts in the sand for each contestant. Give each player a spoon and a bowl. At the signal, they run across the room to the sand pile, dig out their peanuts, put them in the bowl, and return.

Rowing Race: Five people from each beach. They stand in single file, close together, each grasping the forearms of the player in front by extending the arms on either side of that player. When the players are in position, the signal is given, and they walk to a given point and back, working their arms like pistons all the way. The first team to cross the line wins.

Sailboat Race: Stretch a string across the room for each contestant. On each string place a paper sail. The contestant is to blow this "boat" from one end of the string to the other.

Refreshments—Clam Chowder*, Rolls*, iced tea.

A BACKWARD PARTY

Wear clothing backward. Greeting on arrival—"Goodbye," "Goodnight."

Spelling Bee: Words spelled backward.

Backward Begging: Each girl is supplied with a stick of candy. Each boy must ask for it without directly doing so. Veiled and backward hints ought to do the trick.

Backward Races: 1. Walk backward to a given point. 2. On all fours and stiff-legged, back up to a given point.

Backward Charades: Groups alternate in presenting charades of words containing the syllable *back* or *bac*. Examples: bacteria, baccalaureate, backfire, background, backfield, quarterback, halfback, fullback, horseback, tobacco, backing, comeback, backboard.

Backward Games: Play some familiar games with players being required to move backward—Going to Jerusalem, Fruit Basket Turnover, Drop the Handkerchief.

Refreshments—Ice-cream sundaes and soft drinks.

Say "Howdy" instead of "Goodnight" and back out.

A CLOWN PARTY

Urge everyone to come in clown costume. For those who fail to dress appropriately, have on hand clown hats and collars made of crepe paper, together with a supply of grease paint. Everyone should be decorated in approved clown style, face included.

Decorations—The room can be given a festive appearance with a plentiful supply of toy balloons, Japanese lanterns, and serpentine and crepe-paper streamers.

Program

Four Clowns in a Row: Give each person a sheet of paper marked off in twenty squares. In each square guests must obtain the signature of another guest. This means that each person will get the signatures of twenty people, one for each square. Provide each player with fifteen or twenty small stickers, available in "office and school supply" departments. Clown faces might be painted on them.

Each guest is now asked to write his or her own name on a small piece of paper. These are placed in a hat. The leader draws the names from the hat one at a time. As a name is called, the person bearing it responds with a lusty "Here," and raises the right hand. This serves as an introduction to the group. Guests who have that name on their papers put a sticker in the square where it appears.

Any player who gets four stickers in a row, either across, down, or diagonally, shouts, "Four clowns in a row!" and reads off the names. Some suitable award may be made to that player.

William Tell Stunt: The leader announces that two of the clowns will put on a William Tell archery exhibition. The two clowns appear. An apple is placed on the head of one of them with careful precision. "William," with his bow and arrow, then paces off about ten steps and turns to aim. As soon as his back was turned, the other clown had removed the apple from his head and taken a healthy bite out of it. "William" patiently returns and places the apple back in position. Again he paces off, and again a bite is taken out of the apple. With a shrug of the shoulders, "William" proceeds to again place it in position. This time the other clown removes the apple and hastily finishes it. He then rushes from the room with William Tell in pursuit. No words are spoken.

A Clown Duel: Two clowns appear with stick swords. In the end of each stick is a pin. The swordsmen have several inflated balloons inside their clown suits. Sharp thrusts are made which puncture the balloons one by one. When all the balloons are punctured, the clowns shake hands, embrace, and retire arm in arm. Much of the fun will

depend upon the way the clowns pantomime the burlesque
duel.

Clown Chariot Race: Ten contestants to each group and
one chair to each group. Contestants stand in single file,
the two lines eight to ten feet apart. The first player in each
line has a chair. At the signal it is passed overhead to the
player behind. That player passes it back overhead to the
next, and so on to the end of the line. When the last player
receives the chair, he or she sits down, and the two players
just ahead drop back and carry that player, chair and all, to
the head of the line. The two carriers then hurry back to
their position at the foot of the line. The player who has just
been carried to the head of the line starts the chair down
the line again. So it goes until every player has been
carried in the chariot to the head of the line, and the
original first player is back in position.

Clown Hat Pitch: Form two teams. Two clown hats are
placed on the floor, open side up. Each person is given three
peanuts. From a distance of about fifteen feet, each in turn
tries to toss the peanuts into his or her team's hat. After all
players have thrown, the peanuts in each hat are counted,
and the side with the largest total wins.

Clown Volleyball: A row of chairs across the room serves
as a net. Alternate them, the first facing one way, the next
the other. Two toy balloons of different colors are used as
volleyballs. Both sides serve at the same time, thus
putting both balls in play. The balls do not need to go over
the net on the serve. The other players may help knock it
across. A player may hit a ball twice or more in succession.
The ball is in play as long as it is up in the air. It is out of
play when it hits a chair or the floor. A side scores when a
ball is grounded in the territory of the opponents. When
one of the balls is grounded, the sides continue to play with
the other ball. No serve is allowed until both balls have
been grounded.

Any number of players may play. A foul is called if the player reaches over the "net" into the opponents' territory. Fifteen points constitute a game.

Circus Ring Relay: Ten to fifteen players on a side. Two separate circles. Players are seated in chairs facing out from center. One player on each side is designated as starting player. At the signal, these players get up and walk rapidly around their circles, seating themselves in their own chairs when they have completed their rounds. The players on their right get up as soon as their leaders pass and the players to those players' right follow, so that by the time the starters are back in their chairs, more than half of each circle is in motion. The first side to have all its players walk around the circle and sit down wins.

Next try this with the players running. The third time, try it with all the players carrying their chairs with them around the circle. All players must be seated before the team can be considered finished.

Refreshments—Clown cakes and pink lemonade. If a clown cake mold cannot be obtained, round cookies could be given clown faces, using white and red icing.

A GOLF TOURNEY

On arrival, guests apply for tourney scorecards. These cards are arranged in groups. One group is numbered *One,* another *Two,* and so on up to *Nine.* Each group goes to the "Hole" indicated by the number on the scorecard. "Holes" are designated by large numbers on standards.

Ten minutes is allowed at each game. The starter's whistle indicates starting and quitting time for each round. Groups progress to the next hole after each game.

Hole 1: Driving. Tin can sunk in ground. Golf club or broomstick. Golf ball, or large marble. Each person has a turn to see how many strokes are necessary to put the ball in the hole.

Hole 2: Beanbag Board. How many shots necessary to toss beanbag through each hole on the board? Ten tries per person.

Hole 3: Ring Toss. Chair legs. How many tosses to get ring on each of the four legs of the chair? Ten tries per person.

Hole 4: Candle Shot. Shoot out a lighted candle with a water pistol. Limit to ten shots. Candle should be five feet from player.

Hole 5: Quiz. Hand out duplicated tests with a row of horizontal numbers: 1, 2, 3, 4, 5, 6, 7, 8. The test follows:
1. If Florida is not south of the Mason/Dixon line, write the letter *R* under 4. If it is, write the letter *B* under 1.
2. If a rabbit runs faster than a man, write *N* under 6. If not, write T under 7.
3. If iron cannot be made to float on water, write *X* under 8. If it can, write the letter *O* under 2.
4. If refrigerators were invented in 1865, write *Y* under 5. If not, write the letter *O* under 4.
5. If an airplane can take off against the wind, write *G* under 5. If not, write *S* under 1.
6. If cactus does not grow in Arizona, write *I* under 3. If it does, write *A* under 7.
7. If blackberries are red when they are green, write *L* under 3. If not, write *F* under 8.
8. If the Great Divide is in the Catskill Mountains, write *K* under 2. If it is in the Rocky Mountains, make a period under 8.
9. If you like lots of what this spells, help yourself. If not, the same to you!

ANSWER

1	2	3	4	5	6	7	8
B	O	L	O	G	N	A	

Insist that players work rapidly at these tests. After five or six minutes call time and read the correct answers. The game may be played by simply reading each question and pausing a moment for players to write their answers on cards or paper.

Hole 6: Dart Board. Concentric circles, 1 at center, 2 next, then 3 outside circle. Missing the board counts 5. Smallest score wins.

Hole 7: Ball Toss. Nail tin can or cup to a stick two feet long. Attach golf ball or rubber ball to string and tie to end of stick. Players toss ball into air and attempt to catch it in cup. Ten tries. Each miss scores one point.

Hole 8: Funnel Catch. Players bounce a tennis ball against the wall and catch it on the rebound in a funnel. Ten tries. One point for each miss.

Hole 9: Ball Bounce. Players bounce rubber ball into a wastebasket or bucket. Five tries. One point for each miss.

A "caddie" is in charge of each "Hole" to give instructions, keep game moving, help players with their scores, and see that they move on to the next game as soon as the whistle blows. The smallest score wins.

Refreshments—Chocolate Pie* and beverage.

A LEMON-SQUEEZE PARTY

Here is a novel party that will be lots of fun. Each guest is asked to bring one lemon. Extra lemons may be furnished for guests who forget. Ice, water, and sugar are provided. The group is organized so that everyone has some duty to perform. Some cut the lemons, some squeeze them, others make the lemonade, others prepare the ice. Two persons are assigned the job of putting the seeds in a jar after counting them. They keep their count secret. Still others are assigned the job of cleaning up and getting the glasses ready for serving.

Lemon Bowling: Set up tenpins, duck pins, or pop bottles. Bowl with a lemon.

Lemons and Lemonade: Guests pair off and hand each other "lemons"—that is, remarks that are not so complimentary. The one to whom the remark is made is to come back with some interpretation that turns the point of the remark, thus making "lemonade" out of the "lemon." For instance, one young man says to his partner, "What a long nose you have." Immediately the young lady responds, "Oh, thank you. Long noses are signs of intelligence. But my, what big feet you have!" "Yeah! All well-built structures have strong foundations." After each exchange of "lemons," players seek new partners.

Lemon Seed Guessing: Have each guest (except the ones who counted them) guess the number of seeds collected. Give a prize to the person who comes closest—a bag of lemons.

Lemon Relay: Divide into equal teams. First member rolls a lemon with the nose from starting line to finish line. Pick up lemon, return to next player.

Refreshments—Lemon Pie* and lemonade.

COUNTY FAIR

Publicity—Posters, handbills, phone committee.

∽ Handbill ∼
(Name of Organization) County Fair
Exhibits   Shows
Fun and Frolic
Don't miss this grand event
Come yourself
and bring your friends
(Date)
7: 30 P.M.

Decorations—Booths, stands, sideshows.

Program—Barkers will be needed to move the crowd from place to place for the various attractions. If there is to be a stage show, an announcer will be needed, also. There should be a chairperson in charge of each of the features—exhibits, sideshows, stage show, booths, etc.

Exhibits: Handcrafts, hobbies, sewing, needlework, old relics. Put someone in charge of this and work it up diligently. It can be a main feature of the program.

Dolls of Many Lands: Have a Doll Show in which children of the organization are invited to put their dolls on display.

Baby Show: People are made up to represent babies. Each baby will have a nurse or a fond mamma to stand proudly by while the nurse and doctor put the troupe through several tests: (a) Weight Test—Place a piece of elastic under arms. Nurse pulls up and announces some ridiculous weight. (b) Bawling Contest. (c) Beauty Contest. Call some man up to pin the blue ribbon on the winner. Just as he stoops to perform this service, all the babies shout, "Da-da."

Sideshows
1. Dancing Midgets (see the Great Grinmore Circus)
2. Fat Lady. A fat man dressed up with extra pillows, etc.
3. Strong Man. Performs amazing feats with fake weights.
4. Fortunetelling. Fortunes with tea leaves. Palm reading.
5. Concert. Some good musical numbers by members of a quartet. "Come to the Fair" would be appropriate for everyone to sing.
6. Swing Your Partner. A folk game demonstration, in costume, if possible.

7. Puppet Show. Marionettes.
8. Athletic Carnival. Events such as Three-Legged Race, Nail Driving Contest, Cracker Eating Relay, etc.
9. Strolling Musicians. Musicians (accordion, violin, harmonica, guitar) who stroll along the midway will add a lot to the enjoyment of the occasion.

Booths: Pie-Eating Contest; Seed-Spitting Contest; Balloon Bust, with darts; Fishing booth; Balloon Art and Helium Balloons; Clown Make-up booth; Cake Walk; Ring Toss; Softball into Milk Cans; Bob for Apples; Weight Guessing booth (need scales); Age Guessing booth; Candied Apple booth; Popcorn and/or Cotton Candy booth.

Refreshments—Corndogs, soft drinks, and other items from the various booths.

A ROLLER-SKATING PARTY

Rent a roller rink just for your group. Here are some ideas for a variety of skating activities:

All Skate: Begin with this activity. It allows time for everyone to arrive, and early arrivers can get started immediately.

Girls Only; Boys Only: Allow three to five minutes for each group several times during the evening.

Grand March: Have the boys line up on one side of the rink and the girls on the other. A boy skates out and meets a girl and they skate down the center of the rink. Everyone follows suit. The first couple circles to the right, the second to the left. The first and second couple meet in the middle and join hands, creating a foursome. The others follow suit. This continues until eight couples meet.

Paper-bag Couples: Have couples skating. Those who are not skating are given small paper bags. The bags are blown up and the tops twisted to hold in the air. A person not skating chooses a couple skating and pops the bag on the back of one of the individuals. He or she then skates with the new partner. The person losing a partner goes to the leader, gets a paper bag, blows it up, and hunts for a new partner.

Threesomes: Two boys with a girl in the center, or vice versa, skate around the rink until a whistle is blown. The person in the center skates forward to new partners. Also try having the threesomes reverse direction when the whistle is blown.

Races: It is best not to race boys against girls, since boys skate faster and tend to be more rough. For markers, use a pliable item.

1. Circle Race. Race by age groupings and sex. Skate around the markers on the rink one to five times.
2. Figure 8 Race. By adding markers, have skaters follow a figure 8 pattern.
3. Partner Race. Skaters squat down, holding onto their own skates, while their partners push them around the course.
4. Choo-choo Race. Four skaters get into squatting position, each holding onto the waist of the person in front. The fifth skater pushes the group around the course.
5. Auto Race. The skater pushes an automobile tire around the course.
6. Skateboard Race. One partner sits on a skateboard; the other partner pushes him or her around the course.
7. Sock Race. The last race can take place when all skates are removed. Once around the floor is a good race in socks. Have a girls' race and a boys' race.

Refreshments—Soft drinks and french fries.

OLD TIMERS' PARTY

Get out the old-fashioned costumes and the old clothes and dress up as an "old-timer." Borrow some spectacle frames. Powder your hair or make a wig. Let's all be old-timers for a night!

Make-up could be provided by the group putting on the party: cold cream; grease paint; brown, gray, white, and crimson liners; white powder. Hair can be whitened by powdering with cornstarch. Crepe hair and spirit gum could be used for beards, sideburns, mustaches. Ordinary hemp rope can sometimes be used for making beards. Teeth can be blacked out with charcoal, black wax, or even carbon paper.

Everybody Make Up: Provide a make-up room and let part of the fun be that of making-up. Encourage young people to use their own creative ability in their characterizations.

Grand Mixer: Guests mill around getting acquainted with one another and introducing themselves with old-time names: Hiram, Charity, etc.

Play Old-time Games: Charades, Wink, Going to Jerusalem, It, Old Dan Tucker, and Brown-eyed Mary; or some newer games: One Frog, It's a What?, Buzz-Fizz, Scissors.

Sing Old-time Songs: "Silver Threads Among the Gold," "When You and I Were Young, Maggie," "Annie Laurie," "Old Folks at Home," "Sweet Alice Ben Bolt," "Love's Old Sweet Song," "Juanita," "In the Gloaming." Some newer songs of the 50s, 60s, 70s can be fun. Check recently published fun song books, or *The New Fun Encyclopedia,* Vol. IV, *Skits, Plays, and Music.*

Refreshments—Lemonade and Strawberry Layer Cake*.

A PAUL REVERE COLONIAL PARTY

On the night of April 18, 1775, Paul Revere made his famous ride.

Invitations—The invitations can be written on "firecrackers." (Paste together two narrow strips of red cardboard, with a piece of string, representing the fuse, protruding at one end.)

> Listen, my children, and you shall hear
> Of a party in honor of Paul Revere.
> A colonial party, a joyful affair,
> So dress up in costume; be sure to be there.

Decorations—Use the colonial colors, buff and blue. Crepe-paper streamers and flowers in these colors can be used effectively. From chandeliers and doorways hang balls of tiny American flags. These can be made by sticking the flags into potatoes.

If Progressive Paul Revere is played, tables should be decorated to represent forts. These can be bricks covered with red paper. At one end attach a pennant bearing the name of the fort or town, and at the other end, an American flag of suitable size. Suggested names: Fort Ticonderoga, Fort William Henry, Fort Duquesne, Boston, Medford, Charlestown, Lexington, Concord.

It would add much to the enjoyment of the occasion if guests would come dressed in colonial costume. If this seems impractical for your crowd, have a committee dressed in colonial style to receive the guests as they arrive.

Program

Paul Revere in Hiding: About the room, hide cards bearing the letters that appear in the name Paul Revere, one letter to each card. There should be at least ten full sets of these cards, with numerous extra cards for each letter except one. This will be the secret key letter and there will be just ten of that letter. For instance, there might be just ten Vs. That would mean that only ten persons could spell the complete name Paul Revere. No player can take other letters until he or she has found the first letter in the name. Secrecy must be observed among the players. The first player to spell the name may be awarded some prize. The ten players to find the complete Paul Revere may be awarded crepe-paper cockades of red, white, and blue. These are worn during the evening.

Historical Art: Each guest is given paper, pencil, and five minutes in which to sketch an original drawing of some historical event. "Paul Revere's Ride," "Washington Crossing the Delaware," "The Spirit of '76," and "A Colonial Sentinel" are some suggestions. The more ridiculous the pictures, the better. At the end of five minutes they are to be passed to the persons on the right. After inspecting the pictures these persons give them titles of their own choosing. No players are to label their own pictures.

Take the Town: Players are divided into two equal groups. One group is named the Yankees, the other the Redcoats. Chairs are placed in a large circle, facing out. Players march around the room, as far from the circle of chairs as space will permit. When the music stops the players rush for seats. No player is allowed to move a chair in order to get it away from another player. There must be fewer chairs than players. Each time a player left without a chair drops out, one chair is removed. The game continues until all players but one are eliminated. This one is declared winner and is appropriately decorated with a cockade. Those Yankees and Redcoats who drop out are expected to cheer for their teammates who are still in the game. The side having the winner is credited with "taking the town."

Flag Race: Five players represent each side. They are lined up single file. At the opposite end of the room are two potatoes, one for each team, with American flags stuck in them. The first player runs to the flag, snatches it, brings it back, and hands it to the next player, who takes it back, and stands it erect in the potato. This player then rushes back and touches the next teammate, who goes after the flag. This continues until the last player has run. The players of the team that finishes first are decorated with cockades.

Bridling Paul Revere's Horse: This is played like the old game of Pinning the Tail on the Donkey. The players are blindfolded one at a time and given a small bridle. The three to pin it nearest the proper place are awarded cockades.

"How?": The Yankees and the Redcoats face one another again in two lines about four or five feet apart. A captain is chosen for each side. Each player is given a word which denotes some action that can be pantomimed or demonstrated. These words are to be arranged in alphabetical order, there being one player for each letter, except that the less commonly used letters may be omitted, if desired. The words are whispered to the player by the captains.

The game starts with the Yankee captain approaching the Redcoat lines and saying, "Paul Revere crossed the river tonight to Charlestown." The opposing captain asks, "How?" The Yankee captain responds, *"A."* The Yankee player whose word begins with *A* steps from the ranks and proceeds to act out the word. If that player can cross the intervening space between the two lines in this manner and get back to the Yankee line before the captain of the Redcoats can guess the word, the player is safe. For instance, *A* may stand for *anxiously, awkwardly, aimlessly,* or some other word beginning with *A.* If the Redcoat captain guesses correctly, the player is captured and is taken behind the enemy lines.

The Redcoats now take their turn. "I understand Paul Revere threw some of the tea overboard during the Boston Tea Party," says the Redcoat. "How?" asks the Yankee captain. "*A*" is again the answer. This time, perhaps it is *angrily,* and the Redcoat with that word crosses No Man's Land, registering anger by looks and actions.

So it goes on down the line. At the end of the game the side with the largest number of prisoners wins, and the winning captain is decorated with a cockade.

The same statement may be made each time or it may be varied at the discretion of the captains. The words must be taken in alphabetical order. Opposing players may suggest words to their captain, but only the captain can capture a player by calling the word. Suggested words:

> *B*—boldly, blandly, briskly
> *C*—courteously, cunningly, coldly, carefully
> *D*—devoutly, discreetly, dignifiedly
> *E*—earnestly, enthusiastically, excitedly
> *F*—fearfully, falteringly, facetiously
> *G*—genially, galloping, gallantly
> *H*—haltingly, haughtily, hysterically
> *I*—idiotically, idly, impassionately
> *J*—jauntily, jubilantly, jeeringly
> *K*—kindly, knavishly, knowingly
> *L*—lamely, lazily, lightly
> *M*—merrily, mincingly, magnificently
> *N*—noiselessly, nonsensically
> *O*—outlandishly, optimistically
> *P*—passionately, patriotically, pleasantly
> *Q*—quickly, quarrelsomely
> *R*—recklessly, revengefully, radiantly
> *S*—savagely, saucily, slyly
> *T*—tearfully, tenderly, thoughtfully
> *U*—uproariously, urgently
> *V*—vampirishly, vindictively, voraciously
> *W*—warily, weakly, whistling
> *Y*—yelling, yearning
> *Z*—zealously, zigzagging

Progressive Paul Revere: Wooden cubes can be obtained from some carpenter shop. The letters R-E-V-E-R-E should be printed with pencil or ink—one letter on each side of the cube. Six cubes make a set. For a small crowd there should be only four players to a table. Players draw slips or tally cards to determine how they shall be placed. For instance, "Company A, Fort Ticonderoga," and "Company B, Fort Ticonderoga," would each appear on two cards. These players immediately go to the table with a Fort Ticonderoga flag.

For larger groups, from six to a dozen players may be assigned to a table. In this case there should be several sets of cubes for each table so it will not be so long between turns. If there are six players to a table, three players will form a company. The companies will remain intact throughout the play of the evening. The company with the largest score is declared winner and cockades are awarded the members. Winning teams at each table progress to the next table, moving clockwise.

No score is allowed unless the player turns up at least the first three letters of the name: R-E-V. This counts ten points. R-E-V-E counts fifteen. R-E-V-E-R counts twenty. A player spelling the entire name is awarded thirty points. Any player who tosses three Vs cancels his or her entire score up to that point in that game.

A bugle call announces the time for the winning companies to advance and attack the next fort or town.

The Winners: A count should be made of the number of cockades won by Yankees and Redcoats, and the victorious group announced. The victorious army should be permitted to parade triumphantly about the room, the officers leading the way.

Refreshments—Layer cake in red, white, and blue layers; ice-cream mounds with tiny American flags stuck in them.

FOOTBALL PARTY

Decorations—Hang school banners and pennants around the room, carrying out two school names and color schemes. Place goal post at each end of room. Give each guest a novelty football on a ribbon. Distribute pieces of brown paper and pins and let the guests make football helmets to wear throughout the evening. Consider your leader the referee and have him or her wear a striped shirt.

Program

Football Spell: Divide group into two teams and have each elect a quarterback. Play animated alphabet using football terms for words to spell. Suggestions: yard, tackle, end, half, jump, down, reverse, forward, guard, back, kick, punt, umpire, timer, quarter, linesman, veterans, wedge, expert, victory, zero, zigzag, zone.

Table Football: An ordinary dining-room table or any such table not over eight feet long will do for this game. Use a ping-pong ball for the football. The ball is put in the center of the field. The players gather around the table, one team on each side, their chins level with the edge of the table. At the sound of the referee's whistle all players begin to blow. If the ball goes outside or over the side of the table the referee retrieves it, places it back in the middle of the field at the point from which it went out, and blows the whistle for the game to continue. Players must not get their faces into the field on penalty of fouling, in which case their opponents will be allowed a free blow by one player of their choice. Each ball that goes off the table at the opponents' end counts one point. Eleven points, fifteen points, or twenty-one points, as decided before play begins, constitute a game.

Variations: (a) Play the same way, using a balloon.

(b) Use a ping-pong ball, but set up pencils as goalposts eight inches apart, using spools as standards for the posts.

One player at a time blows, the ball being placed at center and the player blowing from behind his or her goalpost. A ball that goes through the goalposts counts a touchdown and six points. One over the line but not through the posts counts two points. The sides alternate, and when eleven players have blown for each side, it is half-time.

(c) Use an empty eggshell instead of a ping-pong ball.

Forward Pass: Each player is given three peanuts. A basket is provided for each side. Players stand ten feet from the basket and try to toss peanuts into it. The side having the largest number of peanuts in the basket wins.

Touchdown: Players are seated in two separate circles, facing out, an equal number in each circle. When the referee blows the whistle the leaders on each team start walking around their circles. As soon as they pass the persons on their right, those players follow. And so it goes until all the players have been all around the circle and are seated in their original places. Next, let the players run. The third time, have the players pick up their chairs and carry them with them.

Player Guess: Have a leader read out names of prominent football players and give a prize to the person who names the most correct schools or teams for which they play.

Refreshments—Popcorn, peanuts, and soft drinks.

ALL NIGHT PARTY

This is the type of event any group of youths will enjoy, and any theme may be used.

In a Wild West Party, use a western theme throughout the night, with campfire singing, rodeos, Indian lore, water-pistol duels, stagecoach rides, old western movies, a barbeque cookout.

Capitalize on various aspects of the theme of whatever amusement park is near you, with a Six Flags Over _____?_____ Party.

Ideas for things to do: roller-skating, ice-skating, midnight or early morning hike with breakfast cookout, bowling, swimming, movies, lots of relay games, volleyball, basketball, novelty sports.

Publicity—Announcements; posters depicting the theme; a large cardboard refrigerator box with a small hole, so people can peek in and see the announcement written inside; a helium-filled balloon with the information on it, floating near the ceiling.

Program for a Disney World Party—During the evening, each activity takes place in one of Disney World's make-believe lands—Fantasyland, Tomorrowland, Frontierland, etc. Dress casually for the evening. Here is a schedule of events:

7:00 P.M.—*Banquet in Frontierland:* Eat at a western type restaurant or have an old-fashioned barbeque cookout. Have western music entertainment.

9:00 P.M.—*Arrive at the Magic Kingdom:* Decorate the entrance by constructing Cinderella's Castle out of mattress boxes. To enter into the Magic Kingdom, everyone must go through the gate. Have a variety of hats available. Hats such as Mickey Mouse ears or coon-skin caps can be purchased from a novelty store or advertising distributor.

9:45 P.M.—*Fantasyland:* This is the time when active games may be played. Suggestions:
1. Mad Hatter's Tea Party Relay: Divide the group into two or more teams. In front of each team, place items of clothing along the relay path. All items need to be extra large to fit over clothing worn by the players: large pair of

pants with a rope for a belt, large pair of boots, large coat, hat, umbrella which must be opened. On the signal, the first player on each team races to the item, puts it on, races to the next item, puts it on, etc., until the course has been completed. At the end of the course is a table containing four crackers. The player is to eat the crackers, pour and drink a glass of tea, then take off and return each item of clothing to its place before returning to the starting line. Then the next player repeats the same procedure.

2. Twenty Thousand Leagues Under the Sea Relay: Have each team select one person to represent it in bobbing for apples. Be sure the stems are off the apples. The first to get an apple wins for his or her team.

3. Mr. Toad's Ride: Each team selects two males who will pull a blanket with a fair maiden on it from a starting point, around an object, and back again.

10:30 P.M.—*Tomorrowland:* Make arrangements for the use of a swimming pool for the next two hours. Floating in water is like walking in space.

1:00 A.M.—*Adventureland:* Decorate a room in the church, a basement, a garage, or a recreation room in a home with a Polynesian motif. Serve fresh fruit (pineapple chunks, cantaloupe and watermelon slices, sliced bananas and apples, sectioned oranges), cold cuts (bologna, ham, turkey), cheese, a variety of breads, condiments, and tomatoes, with fruit punch or soft drinks. Add to the atmosphere with flowers, greenery, and Hawaiian music.

2:00 A.M.—*Main Street, U.S.A.:* Check with a bowling alley and schedule bowling, or with a skating rink for roller-skating during this time. If not available, show old movies made in the early part of the century.

4:00 A.M.—*Libertyland:* In Disney World, the Haunted Mansion is located near the Hall of the Presidents. Make a haunted house for this event. For ideas, see A Haunted House Party in "Fun with Seasonal Celebrations—

October." Conclude the party with an early morning breakfast at the Haunted Mansion.

A BOHEMIAN PARTY

Decorations—Old lanterns and candlesticks, including old bottles, an artist's easel. Weird, funny, and senseless pictures. A few daubs of various brilliantly colored paints in futuristic design may be given the title "Peace at Dawn." All but one of these pictures should be titled. That one is the "unnamed picture." Guests could wear artists' smocks or "beatnik" outfits reminiscent of the 60s.

Program

Sketching: Have each person sketch the person on the right. Sign names of subject and of artist. Pass around for crowd to see.

Chewing Gum Sculpture: Give each person a card and a stick of chewing gum. Guests are to chew the gum and then mold some "work of art" on the card. These should be placed on exhibit.

Naming the Picture: Have each person make up a title for the unnamed picture. Select certain ones to suggest to the group for its decision as to the winner.

Poetry: Give four rhyming words such as *shove, dove, love, above* and ask each person to write a poem, ending the lines with these four words in any order. For a large crowd divide into three or more groups and let each group present a poem.

Soap Carving: Ask each person to bring a bar of Ivory soap and a pocket knife. Have a supply of magazines on hand so the sculptors may consult them for models. Put the results of the modeling contest on display. Information on this art may be found in the library. Or if someone who is expert at soap carving could demonstrate and offer the group some instruction, it would add interest and value to this feature. Be sure to cover the floor with old newspapers.

Bohemian Orchestra: The players use dish mops and pans, a scrubboard, a floor mop, and other such articles. The pianist strikes up some melody and all the players keep time. The pianist gets faster and so do the players. As the pianist slows down so do the players. The tempo gets slower and slower until the climax when the whole group of players yawns and drops off to sleep.

Bohemian Chorus: Records of the well-known songs from *The Student Prince* could be played. Or there could be a good rousing sing, using songs like "Du Liegst Mir in Herzen," "Alouette."

Refreshments—Orangeade and cookies. Try Peanut Blossoms*.

A PROGRESSIVE LAWN PARTY

The possibilities in progressive parties are almost limitless—skill games, mental games, puzzles, creative activities (crafts, sketching, painting, informal dramatics), and other activities. Mark each table or game with its number plainly in view. Type or print directions for each game when directions are needed. Provide tally cards, properly numbered, to indicate groupings.

Methods of Progression:

1. Four players at each activity. Two winners progress. Two losers go to last activity. Change partners each time.

2. Even number at each activity. Half of the group progresses.

3. Entire group progresses to new game. In this case players are in one group all evening.

4. Entire group progresses, half moving forward to the next activity and the other half backward to the next activity, except Table 1. Half of Table 1 goes to the last

table and half to the table immediately ahead. Thus if there are ten tables, half of Table 1 goes to Table 10 and half to Table 2. Also, half of the last table goes to Table 1 and half to table just behind.

5. Progress when (a) game or activity is finished; (b) leader rings a bell; or (c) couple at head table finishes an activity.

Program

Clock Golf: Dig twelve holes in a circle thirty feet in diameter, around a center hole. Players start at center and putt to hole No. 1 (as on a clock face) at circumference. Then putt back to center, then to hole No. 2, etc., until each player has completed the full round. The number of strokes in making the circuit are counted.

Beanbag Golf: Toss a beanbag into cans, buckets, baskets, and boxes over a course of nine holes, and return.

Muffin Pan Toss: Toss a small disc into a muffin tin from a distance of six feet. Each cup is numbered, indicating the score. Discs may also be numbered, in which case getting a disc in its proper receptacle doubles the score.

Washer Pitching: Dig five holes—one in each corner and one in the center—and sink five small soup cans. Players score ten points for tossing washer into center hole and five points for each of the corners. Toss from a distance of ten to fifteen feet.

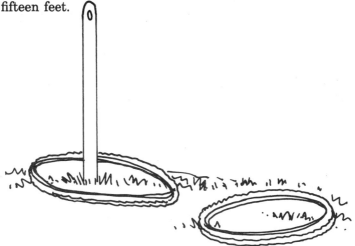

Pole Ring Toss: Drive broom-handle stakes into the ground so that they stand about two or two-and-a-half feet above ground. Make eight rings, four red and four black, seven to eight inches in diameter, of old bicycle tires. Players toss rings from a distance of fifteen or twenty feet. Each ringer counts one point. Fifteen or twenty-one points, as agreed, constitute a game. Each player throws four rings, tossing alternately, as in Horseshoes.

Hole Bowl: Holes are dug in the ground large enough to sink coffee cans (about five inches in diameter), one in each hole. There should be six holes, arranged in triangle shape as in bowling. These holes are one foot apart and are numbered for their values: back row, three holes, 75, 100, 50; second row, two holes, 25, 35; front, one hole, 10. Players bowl from a distance of fifteen feet, using croquet balls. If a player "calls" a shot and makes good, the score is doubled for that shot. For instance, if the player announces, "I am bowling for 100," and then proceeds to bowl the ball into 100, the score is 200. But that player cannot call 100 again during that turn, even though it was missed the first time. If a player calls a shot and misses but goes into another hole, the score is whatever that hole allows. It would be advisable to erect a three- or four-inch-high backstop a foot or so in back of the last can to stop balls that are tossed too hard.

Chair-leg Ring Toss: Turn a chair or stool upside down. Players try to ring the legs with rope rings five inches in diameter. Five points for each ringer. Toss from a distance of six to eight feet.

Refreshments—A variety of chips and dips, with cold soft drinks.

A NEWSPAPER PARTY

Invitations—Make a poster by tearing a jagged hole out of a newspaper and pasting the newspaper on a piece of posterboard. In the hole, print the announcement of the party.

Decorations—Rig up a newsstand in one corner of the room, displaying copies of magazines. Use newspapers for tablecloths, and make other decorations out of newspapers.

Program

Newsboys: Begin by having a couple of "newsboys" suddenly appear, shouting "EXTRA!" as they pass out sheets containing the program.

Newspaper Hats: Have each person make a newspaper hat to wear during the evening. Furnish paper, pins, and as many pairs of scissors as you can.

Advertisements: Cut out of magazines and newspapers familiar advertisements, deleting the name of the product. Number these and place them about the room. Provide players with pencil and paper and have them guess the products advertised. The "Extra" given out earlier in the evening may contain space for these answers.

Newspaper Doilies: Each player is given a page from a newspaper and a few moments to tear out some design for a doily. The best of these designs may be put on display.

Newspaper Race: Contestants are furnished two sheets of newspaper. These they must place on the floor and step from one to the other as they race down the course. This means they will have to take a step and then reach back for the sheet they have just left to place ahead of them. Under no circumstances must their feet touch anything but the newspapers. Naturally, they will make slow progress.

Newspaper: Allow five minutes for each person to make as many words as possible out of the letters in the word *newspaper.*

Dramatization: Divide into several groups and have each group dramatize some incident reported in the daily paper. Each group would be furnished with a recent newspaper and the selection of the item left to the group.

The Comic Strip: Each person would be given paper and pencil and required to sketch a likeness of the person sitting to the right. These cartoons are labeled with the names of the persons they are supposed to represent and passed around the group.

Reporting: Slips are passed out which assign the guests to different groups—Sports, News, Editorials, Advertising, Society Page, etc. These groups are given from fifteen to thirty minutes to write up their respective sections of *The Daily Gossip.* This newspaper is then read, each group having someone read its particular section.

Newspaper Costumes: (a) Pair off and have one partner dress the other, consulting the latest fashion magazines, or using their own ideas. A whole newspaper, scissors, and tape are furnished.

(b) In a large crowd it might be advisable to have three or four groups and dress one person in each group.

Refreshments—Serve Cherry-topped Cheese Pie* and coffee or light beverage.

A PUZZLE PARTY

A Puzzling Test: Each guest takes the test immediately upon arrival. Duplicated sheets are provided, with the following questions.

1. If blackberries are green when they are red, write *H* at the right hand side of this test. If not, write *X*.

2. If black cows give white milk that makes yellow butter, write *A* at the right hand side. If not, write *Y*.

3. If a regulation football field is just 90 yards long from goal to goal, write *Z* to the right. If not, write *V*.

4. If paper is made out of wood, write *E* to the right. If not, write a zero.

5. If an airplane can travel faster than an automobile, write *A*. If not, write the number four.

6. If summer is warmer than winter, write *G*. If not, write *R*.

7. If Longfellow wrote "Twinkle, Twinkle, Little Star," write *S*. If not, write *O*.

8. If candy is sweeter than lemons, write *O* in the margin. If not, write the number three.

9. If Beethoven wrote "Moonlight Sonata," write *D* in the margin. If not, write the number four.

10. If the climate in Siberia is warmer than it is in Florida, write *X*. If not, write *T*.

11. If the printing press was first invented by an American, write *Z*. If not, write *I*.

12. If New York City is the capital of New York state, write *A*. If not, write *M*.

13. If baseball is a major sport, write *E* in the margin. If not, write *O*.

When guests have answered each of these questions correctly, they have written

H-A-V-E A G-O-O-D T-I-M-E.

Puzzling Names: Names of certain members of the group are written with jumbled letters—for instance, REPTOR for PORTER. Each person gets a list and tries to straighten out the names. At the end of five minutes, or some other designated time limit, the leader reads a correct list and players check their own answers.

Jigsaws: Tables are provided for jigsaw puzzles. Simple puzzles, Bible pictures, and difficult puzzles can be used. Work out plans so that each guest has an opportunity to work on all types. Four people or more at a given table. Slips are drawn to determine who shall be at what table. Each group is allowed to work ten minutes and then all players move to their next tables. If a puzzle is incomplete, it is left for the next group to finish. Plan so that each person will be with a different group on each move.

Crazy Data Test: Guests are given pieces of paper upon which they write their names. The group is then notified that they must answer the following questions with yes or no, but must give the wrong answers. For instance, if the question were: "Is it hot at the South Pole?" The answer would be yes. About three seconds are allowed after each question. Papers are exchanged and the leader reads the questions and answers.

1. Is it cold at the North Pole? No.
2. Is the moon made of cheese? Yes.
3. Are oranges black in South Dakota? Yes.
4. Does water flow uphill in China? Yes.
5. Does a car use gasoline in the radiator? Yes.

6. Will paper burn upside down? No.
7. Can a dog bark after it is dead? Yes.
8. Are bananas good to eat in Siberia? No.
9. Are lemons sweet in California? Yes.
10. Is rain water good to drink in Honolulu? No.
11. Is gasoline inflammable? No.
12. Are green apples good for indigestion? Yes.
13. Is snow white on a coal pile? No.
14. Is gold valuable when lost? No.
15. Is a sweet potato a vegetable? No.
16. Is baking soda poisonous? Yes.
17. Is strychnine good for baby's colic? Yes.
18. Does kerosene taste good in milk? Yes.
19. Is the bottom of the ocean wet? No.
20. Does the sun set in the north? Yes.

In case there are ties, the following questions are read. Allow about one second after each question.

1. Is the capitol of the United States in New York? Yes.
2. Does the Mississippi River flow north? Yes.
3. Is the Mississippi River closer to Wisconsin than it is to New York? No.
4. Does it ever snow in Nebraska? No.
5. Will ten make a dozen in Florida? Yes.
6. Can eggplants hatch in three weeks? Yes.
7. Do kangeroos brush their teeth after shaving? Yes.
8. Was George Washington born in Minnesota? Yes.
9. Do natives eat crocodiles in Honolulu? Yes.
10. Is molten lava good for toothache? Yes.

Or use the *Recreation "Pop" Test*. Give the guests three minutes in which to complete this test.

1. Read everything before doing anything.
2. Put your name in the upper right hand corner of this paper.
3. Circle the word *name* in sentence 2.
4. Draw 5 small squares in the upper left hand corner of this paper.

5. Put an X in each square.
6. Put a circle around each square.
7. Sign your name under the title.
8. After the title write "yes, yes, yes."
9. Put a circle around each word in sentence 7.
10. Put an X in the lower left hand corner of this paper.
11. Draw a triangle around the X you just put down.
12. On the reverse side of this paper, multiply 703 by 985.
13. Draw a rectangle around the word *paper* in sentence 4.
14. Call out your first name when you get to this point.
15. If you think you have followed directions up to this point, shout, "I have!"
16. On the reverse side of this paper, add 8250 and 7250.
17. Put a circle around your answer. Put a square around the circle.
18. Count out loud, in your normal speaking voice, backward from 10 to 1.
19. Now that you have finished reading carefully, follow the directions in sentences 1 and 2 only.

For extra credit, add the following column of figures aloud as quickly as possible!

$$
\begin{array}{r}
20 \\
1000 \\
10 \\
1000 \\
30 \\
1000 \\
10 \\
20 \\
1000 \\
\underline{10} \\
\end{array}
$$

Puzzling Refreshments—Allow each person to order three items from a menu of five. The guests order by number and do not know what the numbers represent. People are served the three items they have ordered. Of course, those who ordered the wrong things are later given the real refreshments. Here's the menu key: 1, empty plate; 2, piece of cake; 3, glass of water; 4, ice cream; 5, toothpick.

A COUNTRY-WESTERN PARTY

Publicity—"Howdy, and welcome to the wildest, most fun-filled country and western party this side, or any side of the Pecos Wilds." That ought to create a little curiosity from prospective party guests.

Announce that everyone should dress in western outfits (jeans, plaid shirt, bandana around the neck, boots, hat).

Decorations—The room should have a western flavor, with split-rail fences, bales of straw, old wagon wheels, red lanterns hanging from the walls, old barrels, ropes, saddles, etc. Leave plenty of room in the center for games. The refreshment area can have a sign reading Water Hole or Dry Gulch Saloon.

Program—As guests arrive, a live band or taped music can play country-western tunes. Pin on each guest a name-tag cut in the shape of a star. Have red stars, yellow, orange, etc. The color of the star will denote the team each guest will be on when the party begins. Have a judge for each team ready to keep score. There should be no more than four teams. Any number of players can be on each team, but there should be equal numbers of boys and girls.

Boot Hill: Have each team select its most handsome cowboy and two of its most creative cowgirls. Each team is given two rolls of toilet tissue. The cowgirls are to wrap the cowboy like a mummy. They are preparing this cowboy for Boot Hill. At the end of the allotted time, points are given by the judges to the first, second, third, and fourth place mummy. Judge on neatness of the wrap and creativity of the mummy.

Hoedown: Each group chooses the boy with the biggest appetite and the girl who can run fastest. From the corners of the room, the four girls race to the middle, where there is a large bowl filled with regular size marshmallows. Each girl takes one from the bowl, races back to her partner and feeds him the marshmallow. Each cowboy eats it as quickly as he can. The cowgirls race back and forth from the bowl to the cowboys, feeding them marshmallows. The judges must keep count of the marshmallows each cowboy eats. Time limit: one minute. The cowboy who eats or still has in his mouth the largest number of marshmallows wins points for his team.

Bronco Buster: Have one refrigerator box for each team. Players line up behind a box. The first player to "ride the bronco"—a cowboy—places the box over his head (players 2 and 3 may help). On the signal, he is to "ride" (walk or run) from the starting line to a designated point where a judge stops him, turns him around, and sends him back to the starting line. Players 3 and 4 help him out of the box and place the box over the second player's head. Points are awarded to the first through fourth place in this relay.

Ride 'em Cowgirl: Each team lines up with the cowgirls riding piggy-back on the cowboys. They are to race from the starting line, around an object, and back to the starting line. Points are awarded for first through fourth place.

Stampede: Each team should huddle close together. Wrap a clothesline-weight rope around each team and tie it in a knot. Be certain teams are equidistant from one another and from an object in the center of the room. On the signal, teams are to make their way around the object and back home as they stampede together. Points are awarded for first through fourth place.

Git Along Little Doggies: Each team has a broom, a yardstick or dowel rod, and an aluminum drink can. Players are to ride the broom horse, pushing the can with the yardstick, from a starting point, around an object, and back. Each player completes this series. Points for first through fourth place.

Lasso: Each team chooses three players to represent it in the contest. With a rope, each player has three tries to lasso a chair ten feet away. Points are given for each successful attempt.

Tie 'em Up: Each team forms a small circle. Everyone reaches in with the right hand and grasps another person's hand. With the left hand, each player is to grasp the hand of a person other than the one whose hand the player already holds. Without letting go of either hand, the group is to untangle the knot. They are allowed to keep palms together if they need to twist around, but they must stay in contact with one another. Points for first through fourth place.

Gun Fight: Have tables lined up (be sure to place sheets of plastic underneath). On each table, have ten lighted candles. Set up the same number of tables six to eight feet away. Place a pail of water and an empty water pistol on each team's table. On the signal, the first member of each team fills the water gun and takes ten shots at the candles, then the next player in line takes ten shots, and this continues until all candles are out or until all players have had a turn. As the water gun becomes empty, the players simply fill it up again. Teams with the least number of candles still burning after all players have shot win points for first through fourth place.

Point System: After each event, total and announce the standings. Give outrageous scores—up to 100,000 for various events. Deduct points if a team talks during instructions. It will help control the crowd.

Refreshments—Barbecue sandwiches, cole slaw, baked beans, french fries, and soft drinks. Have a country-western band perform. If no band is available, enjoy the fellowship while taped music plays.

FUN WITH FELLOWSHIPS

To differentiate between a party and a fellowship, one need know only why the social event is planned. Most parties usually last from one to six hours, depending on the purpose of the occasion. A fellowship is a short party which takes place either before or after an event, such as a church service or a meeting, and usually lasts less than one hour. Both possess similar features—a mixer or ice breaker, active and inactive games, and refreshments. Both seek to ensure that guests have an enjoyable time as they interact together.

COUNTRY CAPERS

Publicity—Indicate the variety of games to be played at the fellowship. One poster might include a striped barber pole to give an indication that some activity will take place in a barber shop. Another might be in the shape of a mailbox, another a cracker barrel, and so forth. Time, date, and place need to be included on all publicity.

Program

Mixer: As guests arrive, give each of them the name of a song, which they are not to share with anyone. When all have arrived, they are to begin singing their own songs, listening for others who are singing the same song. When all have found their groups, they sit together. Suggested songs: "Old MacDonald Had a Farm," "Clementine," "She'll Be Comin' 'Round the Mountain," "You Are My Sunshine."

Barber Shop: In the center of the room place a table holding the following items: shaving cream, plastic spoon, bowl of warm water, washcloth, towel, after-shave lotion (strong smelling).

Each team is to select a boy, who is to sit in a chair facing his group, and a girl, who stands behind him, blindfolded. She is to put a sheet around the boy's neck (as in a barber shop), find the shaving cream and apply it to the boy's face, then with the plastic spoon handle, shave the boy's face. She finds the washcloth, wets it, washes his face, and dries it with the towel. She then liberally applies the after-shave lotion. A judge is to choose the boy who has the cleanest shave (least amount of shaving cream left on the face).

Post Office: The entire group sits in a large circle. Slips of paper, with the name of a different city written on each, are taped under the seats of all chairs except one. That chair has IT written on the piece of paper. When guests have found their slips, IT goes to the middle of the circle and the chair is removed.

The leader, who has a list of all the cities, shouts that a letter is going from New York to Dallas. The persons occupying the chairs representing those two cities must change seats. IT must attempt to get one of the vacant chairs. If IT succeeds, the other person becomes IT. When the leader shouts "General Delivery," everyone must exchange places.

Refreshments—Have the refreshment corner set up like an old country store, with a cracker barrel full of crackers. On the counter, have a large piece of cheese to slice, apple slices, dill pickles, pretzels, chips and dip. Serve apple cider.

YOU NEVER SAW SUCH A TRACK MEET

Publicity—Using a black felt-tip pen, boldly write the information about the track meet on the sports page of your local newspaper. Make certain *all* pertinent information is included: date, time, place.

Decorations—Before the meet, be sure to gather all equipment needed, mark off the various field-event courts, and make up awards (ribbons made from construction paper or trophies made from paper cups).

Program

Mixer: Choo-Choo. All players stand in a circle facing the center of the room. Four or more players are chosen as team leaders and come to the center. When the signal is given, the leaders approach persons in the large circle and introduce themselves. The persons approached then tell their names. The leaders repeat the others' names in a loud voice five times in rhythm, at the same time sliding forward first the right foot, then the left foot, alternately. Thus if the name were Mary, the pattern would be like this:

Mary	Mary		Mary	Mary	Mary
(R)	(L)		(R)	(L)	(R)

The last three slides are done quickly. The leaders then turn around in place and the persons approached put their hands on their leaders' waists and hang on. The pairs form trains which choo-choo across the room to other players. When the third players have given their names, the other pairs slide their feet and repeat the names five times as above. The players then turn around in place, letting go of each other. The third persons are now part of the trains and the second players are the leaders. The team that has the most people after five minutes is declared the winner.

Once the teams are formed, let them choose names. The names they will come up with may surprise you, but youths have a wild sense of humor.

Track Meet: The names of the events are intentionally misleading. You may substitute your own ideas for these if you wish. Prepare a score sheet for each team:

INDOOR TRACK MEET

Team Name_____ Captain_____

Scorer_____

Events	Girl	Score	Boy	Score	Total
1. Shot Put	____	____	____	____	____
2. Broad Jump	____	____	____	____	____
3. High Jump	____	____	____	____	____
4. 100-yard Dash	____	____	____	____	____
5. Hammer Throw	____	____	____	____	____
6. Javelin Throw	____	____	____	____	____
7. Discus Throw	____	____	____	____	____
8. Volleyball Throw	____	____	____	____	____
9. Pole Vault	____	____	____	____	____
10. Hurdles	____	____	____	____	____
11. Mile Run	____	____	____	____	____
12. Aquatic Dash	____	____	____	____	____
13. Team Relay (all)	____	____	____	____	____

TOTAL TEAM SCORE ____

Each team captain lists the names of a boy and a girl for the first twelve events. Note that the last event is for the entire team. Each team member should compete an equal number of times, if possible.

Award five points for first place, four for second, and so on; if there are only two teams, simply give one point to each winner.

1. Shot Put. Each contestant inflates a paper bag, twists it closed, and throws it as far as possible.

2. Broad Jump. Each contestant smiles. The smiles are measured with a tape measure, and the widest one wins.

3. High Jump. Contestants attempt to blow a feather over a string held six inches higher than their heads.

4. 100-yard Dash. Place stones or walnuts on top of both shoes of the contestant. Each contestant walks (or slides or shuffles) to the finish line without losing the stones or walnuts. If one rolls off, the player must start over. Distance of the race is 100 inches.

5. Hammer Throw. Tape a two-foot piece of string to a ping-pong ball. Contestants hold the end of the string and throw for distance.

6. Javelin Throw. See who can throw a soda straw farthest.

7. Discus Throw. See who can throw a paper plate farthest.

8. Volleyball Throw. Using inflated balloons, contestants throw for distance.

9. Pole Vault. Contestants try to balance a yardstick or broomstick on their chins. Players with the longest times win.

10. Hurdles. Contestants try to snap four tiddly-winks or buttons into a small cup.

11. Mile Run. Each participant eats three dry crackers, then tries to be the first to whistle.

12. Aquatic Dash. One member of a team feeds another member a baby bottle full of water. The first to empty a bottle wins.

13. Team Relay. Any relay may be used. The entire team takes part in this event.

You might like the following ideas better, or you may want to combine some.

1. 1-yard Dash. Measure out one yard of dental floss and put a piece of bubble gum on the end. Place the other end of the floss in the mouth of each contestant (one from each team). Player must chew the floss up to the bubble gum (without touching the floss with the hands), and then chew the gum. The winner is the first one to blow a recognizable bubble.

2. 50-foot Dash. All participants are to measure their feet. The team with the longest measurement wins.

3. Novelty Race. With their noses, contestants push potatoes across an area of about six to eight feet, around a chair, and back to the start. Other teammates will do the same until all the members of a team have gone around and the last person is back at the start.

4. Hurdle Race. Blindfold one or more team members and have them step over objects while blindfolded. Use your imagination here.

Devotional—Use Hebrews 12:1-2 as a springboard. Keep in mind the parallelism found in the track meet, and emphasize running the race of the Christian life.

Refreshments—Old-fashioned lemonade is always refreshing after a good race. Serve this with homemade gingerbread cookies.

Adapted from Bob Sessoms, *A Guide to Using Sports and Games in the Life of the Church* (Nashville: Convention Press, 1976), pp. 79-80, 90-91; and Bob Sessoms, "Indoor Track Meet," *52 Complete After-Game Fellowships,* comp. by Frank Hart Smith (Nashville: Convention Press, 1980), pp. 36-37. Used by permission.

GETTING TO KNOW YOU BETTER

Prior to fellowship time, arrange the chairs in a large horseshoe shape. This allows participants to be able to see everyone. This shape is also recommended for one of the activities.

Mixer: As guests arrive have them sign their names on slips of paper and place them in a container. Give each guest a pencil and a 5 X 7 card with the following grid:

H	E	L	L	O

Instruct each guest to have the card signed by other guests—a different signature for each square. When their cards are full, the guests may be seated.

The leader then draws a name out of the container. If guests have that name on their cards, they mark out that square. The first guest to mark out all squares either vertically, horizontally, or diagonally calls, "Hello!" and wins the contest. As each name is called, have the person stand. Ask those whose names have not been called to stand and introduce themselves after the contest.

Sing a Song: "Country Gardens" is an excellent get-acquainted song. The following actions make the activity more fun. Give yellow squares of paper to those on the right, red to those on the left, and blue to the others.

Words: Hi, everybody! (Yellows stand and wave to reds.)
　　　　Hi, everybody! (Reds stand and wave to yellows.)
　　　　Hi, everybody! (Blues stand and wave to reds and
　　　　　yellows.)
　　　　Hi! Hi! Hi! (All give three loud football cheers.)
　　　　(Repeat)
　　　　(Whistle the next three measures.)
　　　　Hi! Hi! Hi! (Everyone gives three cheers.)
　　　　Hi, everybody! (Do same actions as before.)
　　　　Hi, everybody! Hi, everybody!
　　　　Hi! Hi! Hi!

Country Gardens

Describe Our Leader: On the back of the Hello card or on another sheet of paper, write the name of the leader. Using the first initials of each name, have guests answer four questions. Example: Kenneth E. McNutt

1. What is he like? kind, enthusiastic, meek
2. Where does he live? Knoxville, Europe, motel
3. What is his favorite food? kale, eggs, mustard
4. What are his hobbies? kissing, eating, macrame

Variation: Instead of using the leader's name, have each person write the name of the person on the left and answer the same questions.

Four Fabulous Facts: Divide the group into smaller groups of no more than four to a group. Have the person in each group who is nearest you stand up. These will be the group leaders. Beginning with their leader, guests in each group are to share four fabulous facts about themselves. One of these facts is to be untrue. After the first person has shared these facts, the others in the group try to identify the untrue fact. Then the next person does the same thing until all have shared. Choose one of the most interesting facts from each group to be shared with the entire group.

Devotional—Before the fellowship, enlist someone in the group to tell of his or her own experience in getting to know Jesus better through the years.

Refreshments—Have each guest bring along a favorite dessert. Let each person tell why it is a favorite.

Adapted from Bob and Carolyn Sessoms, *52 Complete Recreation Programs for Senior Adults* (Nashville: Convention Press, 1979), pp. 74-76. Used by permission.

SUPER BOWL

Publicity—This would be a good time to invite youth from another church and/or from an opposing school. Challenge them to come to the super-bowl fellowship to see who is the real champion of ping-pong football. Encourage them to have cheerleaders for their school, and enlist cheerleaders for your youth's school. You will need a referee dressed in a striped shirt and carrying a whistle; you will also need a scorekeeper with a chalkboard.

Using butcher paper, tempera paint, and your imagination, place several banners at key locations. Be sure to give the date, place, and time. Should you invite youth from another church or school, include the challenge in the publicity.

Decorations—Place the school colors and banners of both schools around the walls. Crepe-paper streamers will add to the festive look. Decorate the refreshment table to look like a concession stand at a football stadium.

In the center of the room, place a ping-pong table. Decorate the table to resemble a football field. With one-inch masking tape, line off the field. Place the names of the two teams in the end zone areas. Drinking straws can serve as goalposts (see illustration).

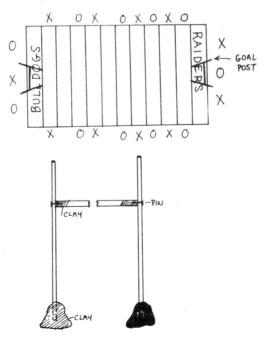

Program—Welcome everyone and play the national anthem.

Ping-pong Football: Rules. Members of the teams sit alternately around the ping-pong table (football field). All players place their hands under the table and must remain seated. The middle player at each end of the table (goal) is the offensive player; the other two players at the end zones are the defensive players (see illustration). Place the ping-pong ball on the fifty-yard line. The referee blows the whistle and everyone begins to blow the ball toward the opponent's goal (where the two defensive players are seated). If the ball rolls off the table, the referee stops play and replaces the ball on the middle of the table at the point where it fell off. A touchdown is made when the ball goes over the opponent's goal. Score six points for each touchdown. Extra points are made by "kicking" the ball through the goalposts with a finger (one point). Have five-minute quarters: Be sure everyone plays even if it takes two games. Substitute freely. Encourage cheering from the cheerleaders. The team with the most points at the end of the game wins.

Devotional—Read Galatians 6:4. Center the devotional thought around some person who is doing his or her best in all of life.

Refreshments—What is better than hot dogs and soft drinks or hot chocolate at a football game? Of course, popcorn, peanuts, and soft drinks work just as well. Serve refreshments from the "concession stand" that has been decorated before the fellowship.

Adapted from Bob Sessoms, "Super Bowl," *52 Complete After-Game Fellowships,* comp. by Frank Hart Smith (Nashville: Convention Press, 1980), p. 54. Used by permission.

INDOOR TRACK MEET

Mixer: Make different colored construction-paper pennants, write team names on the pennants, and attach them to small dowel rods. Give pennants to guests as they enter. Identical large pennants are hanging on the walls (these may be made prior to the fellowship or by early arrivers). Those with pennants alike form groups under the large pennants. Have chairs arranged for the team members, but keep the center of the room open for the field events.

First Event: Team Cheer or Song. Have each team work up a cheer or fight song. Allow about five minutes or longer. Then have each group perform the cheer or song.

Second Event: 100-yard Dash. Provide each team with measuring tape or yardstick. Have everyone remove the right shoe. The leader of each team takes the team's shoes and lines them up heel to toe in the playing field, beginning at a starting line. The team with the longest line of shoes wins the contest. Keep score for first, second, and third place.

Third Event: Standing Broad Grin. With the measuring tape, have each leader measure everyone's smile to see who has the widest smile. This person represents the team in the track meet. Have all contestants come to the center of the room, line up, and be measured. Points are given for first place, second place, and third place.

Fourth Event: Shot Put. Each team selects someone to represent it in this event. Each contestant receives a cotton ball and goes to the starting line. Each one gets three tries to throw the cotton ball like a shot-put. The best of three is the counting distance, and the three players with the best throws win for their teams.

Fifth Event: Hammer Throw. Each team selects a contestant to throw the hammer. The contestants get three throws of the hammer (a two-foot piece of string taped to a ping-pong ball). The contestant, holding the end of the string, twirls the ball around and lets go. The best three distances win points for the players' teams.

Sixth Event: Pole Vault. Another member of each team is selected for the pole vault. See how long each contestant can balance a yardstick in the hand. Award points for first, second, and third place.

Optional Events:
1. Roll ping-pong ball into a can ten feet away.
2. Bounce a tennis ball into a wastebasket.
3. Pitch jar rings over neck of soft-drink bottles.
4. Toss pennies into a muffin pan.
5. Toss badminton birdies into a large juice can.

Devotional—Build a devotional thought based on Galatians 6:4. Stress that it is important to give the best effort in all of life, no matter what the circumstances.

Refreshments—Crackers, cheese, a relish tray, and apple juice.

Adapted from Bob and Carolyn Sessoms, *52 Complete Recreation Programs for Senior Adults* (Nashville: Convention Press, 1979), pp. 76-77. Used by permission.

BARNYARD FELLOWSHIP

Publicity—Announce that at tonight's fellowship there will be a performance by chickens, pigs, and donkeys.

Program

Barnyard Chorus:
1. As participants enter the door, hand each a slip of paper with a drawing of a chicken, pig, or donkey. Be sure to divide the group as evenly as possible.

2. Have each group select a person to serve as choir director.

3. Send each group out to a designated rehearsal room. Allow twenty or thirty minutes for the groups to prepare their renditions of "Old MacDonald Had a Farm," in their particular language: chicken (cluck), pig (oink), or donkey (hee-haw).

4. Have judges available to judge on originality, arrangement, sincerity.

5. Have a tape recorder ready to tape the performances to be played back during the refreshment time.

6. Have the groups return and perform.

7. Announce the judges' decision.

8. Conclude with a mass choir, singing in all the languages.

Refreshments—Be original. Remember the theme: Barnyard. Some ideas: corn on the cob for the pigs, shredded wheat for the donkeys, cornflakes for the chickens.

Adapted from Bob Sessoms, "Barnyard Fellowship," *Fellowships: Plenty of Fun for All,* comp. by Frank Hart Smith (Nashville: Convention Press, 1978), p. 44. Used by permission.

BUBBLE GUM BLOWOUT

Publicity—Announce that there will be FREE BUBBLE GUM at this fellowship.

Program—*Bubble Gum Art:* As guests enter, hand each one two pieces of wrapped bubble gum. Divide into equal groups. With a piece of posterboard, the bubble gum, and the wrappers, have each group design a picture on the posterboard. Allow twenty to thirty minutes. Be sure to discourage human figures.

Have judges view the works of "art" and award only a first-place prize—one piece of bubble gum.

For posterity, take a photograph of each creation.

Refreshments—Root beer or other carbonated drink floats.

Adapted from Bob Sessoms, "Bubble Gum Fellowship," *Fellowships: Plenty of Fun for All,* comp. by Frank Hart Smith (Nashville: Convention Press, 1978), p. 15. Used by permission.

NOAH'S ARK

Publicity

All ye people—
escape the floods by climbing aboard Noah's Ark at

_____,
Friday, September ____,
immediately after the ball game.

Program

Find Your Cage: Duplicate each of the following instructions on separate pieces of paper. Each guest should receive one instruction upon arrival:

1. Fly like a *bird* by flapping your hands like wings and whistling like a bird. Find others doing the same and get together.

2. Look like an *ape* by letting your arms hang loosely in front of you. Swing them back and forth while making a grunting sound. Find others doing the same and get together.

3. Act like an *elephant* by placing your right fist on top of your left fist and placing them against your nose. Find others doing the same and get together.

4. Be a *giraffe* by stretching your neck, extending your arms stiffly down in front of you, and walking on your tiptoes. Find others doing the same and get together.

5. Act like a *hyena* by making a silly grin and laughing in a funny way. Find others doing the same and get together.

6. Prance like a *deer* by opening your hands, placing your thumbs on the sides of your head, and making antlers. Find others doing the same and get together.

After all are in groups, give each group a piece of butcher paper, cardboard or posterboard, and felt-tip pens or crayons. Ask the groups to design their cages. With masking tape, place these on the wall for background.

Animal Rhythm: This game is played with eight to ten players in each group. Sit in a circle on the floor. Assign each player a motion which designates an animal.

1. Deer. Fingers extended like antlers on the sides of the head.

2. Goat. Make a goatee by placing one hand under chin and wiggling fingers.

3. Snake. One hand and arm slithering like a snake.

4. Giraffe. Extend arm up with hand slanted down like a head.

5. Elephant. Make two fists, placing one on top of the other, then on the nose.

6. Fish. Pucker up lips and open and close mouth rapidly.

7. Monkey. Lift one arm up, scratch side, and make a monkey sound.

8. Wolf. Raise chin and howl like a wolf.

9. Alligator. Extend arms in front, right hand (palm down) over left hand (palm up), and make like an alligator by raising and lowering arms.

10. Bird. Make hands flap like wings.

As players pat their knees or the floor in rhythm, the leader begins to do his or her own motion, then one of the other animal motions. The player to whom the second motion was assigned responds by doing his or her own motion, then that of another animal. If a player misses a motion, that player moves to the end of the circle (the leader is on the left) and takes whatever action the last player had; everyone else moves up. Object: to get the leader out.

Kangaroo, Elephant, Fish: All players form one large circle. Instruct them how to represent the kangaroo, elephant, or fish. The person who is IT will point to a person and say "kangaroo," "elephant," or "fish," and count to ten. If IT says "Kangaroo!" the person pointed to will cup hands together at the stomach to form a pouch; the persons on the right and left will jump up and down. If any of the three fail to do their part before IT counts to ten, then they become IT and change places with the leader.

For elephant, the person pointed to places the right fist on top of the left fist, then places them to the nose, making a trunk. The persons to the left and right will each place a hand, palm open and facing out, against each of the elephant's ears.

For fish, the person pointed to will pucker the lips and move them up and down like a fish. The people to the left and right will place their own hands together and wiggle them back and forth like wiggling fish tails.

All making a mistake become IT. Several can be IT at the same time. For variety, make up your own animals and motions.

Devotional—Tell the story of Noah and the Ark in your own words; conclude with a reading of Genesis 9:8-17.

Refreshments—Decorate with animals drawn on paper tablecloths. Serve animal crackers or Brownies* and milk or coffee.

Adapted from *Baptist Youth Kit for Leaders,* 7-76. © Copyright 1976. The Sunday School Board of the Southern Baptist Convention; and Bob Sessoms, "Noah's Ark," *52 Complete After-game Fellowships,* comp. by Frank Hart Smith (Nashville: Convention Press, 1980), p. 39. Used by permission.

COFFEE BREAK OLYMPICS

The coffee break is a routine social event that needs some enthusiasm. Here are several suggestions to liven up the event by doing one activity a week, or trying all of them at an office party.

Wastebasket Toss: Each contestant wads up a piece of paper and tosses it toward a wastebasket. Each piece that goes into the basket scores a point. Try a five-, ten-, or twenty-foot toss. The winner gets a special treat with his or her coffee.

Hat Tree Toss: From several distances, toss a hat at a hat tree. For a more difficult toss, see who can toss the hat on top of the hat tree or on the other side of the tree. The more difficult the toss, the greater the point value. Treat the winner.

Secretary Chair Twirl: In a secretary chair, have the contestants see how many complete circles can be made in ten seconds. Treat the winner.

Coffee Cup Relay: Carrying three cups of coffee at one time, see who can run the course from the coffee machine to the boss' office, without spilling coffee and in the shortest time. Treat the winner.

Refreshments—Ripple Coffeecake* and coffee.

ALL-CHURCH FELLOWSHIP
TRUTH OR CONSEQUENCES

Let the senior adults sponsor an all-church fellowship. In days of yesteryear, there appeared on the radio and later on television an old favorite of senior adults—"Truth or Consequences."

Select a senior adult to preside as the master of ceremonies—to read the question and pronounce the consequence. Like the television version, once the question is asked, the buzzer sounds before the person has a chance to answer. Then the consequence is read.

The timekeeper should have a stopwatch and a buzzer, horn, bell or whistle to indicate that time is up.

From the audience, select persons or groups to come on stage for a question. Use other senior adults to help with the consequences, if needed.

Publicity—Have senior adults go to the various Sunday school rooms to invite everyone to the fellowship. If at all possible, have a senior adult announce the big event from the pulpit on Sunday.

Program—These Bible-related questions are humorous. Here are a few samples.

1. Who was the first man mentioned in the Bible?
Answer: Chap. 1.

2. When is baseball first mentioned in the Bible?
Answer: Genesis 1:1, "In the beginning" (big inning).

3. Who was the fastest runner in history?
Answer: Adam—he was first in the human race.

4. What time of day was Adam born?
Answer: A little before Eve.

5. When was paper money first mentioned in the Bible?
Answer: When the dove brought "green" back to Noah.

6. Who was the most successful doctor in the Bible?
Answer: Job—he had the most patience (patients).

7. Who was the straightest man in the Bible?
Answer: Joseph—Pharaoh made a *ruler* out of him.

8. Who was the greatest actor in the Bible?
Answer: Samson—he brought down the house.

9. What two noblemen are mentioned in the Bible?
Answer: Barren fig tree and Lord how long.

10. How do we know Paul was a pie maker?
Answer: The Bible says he went to Philippi (fill a pie).

Should you not wish to use the above questions, try some of these:

1. Why is the letter W like gossip?

Answer: Because it makes *ill will*.

2. Name the longest word in the English dictionary.

Answer: Smiles—there is a mile between the first and last letters.

3. What type of dress lasts longest?

Answer: A house dress—it never gets worn out.

4. On what row will you find the coldest seats in a theater?

Answer: On Z row (zero).

5. What is worse than raining cats and dogs?

Answer: Hailing taxicabs.

6. Why is your nose not twelve inches long?

Answer: Because it would be a foot.

7. If two are company and three are a crowd, what are four and five?

Answer: Nine.

8. What grows larger as you take more from it?

Answer: A hole.

9. What was the highest mountain before Mount Everest was discovered?

Answer: Mount Everest.

10. What is the center of gravity?

Answer: The letter V.

Here are some consequences:

1. Whistle "Dixie" with your mouth full of crackers.

2. Have several male contestants for this consequence. Ask the wives of these men to feed them using baby bottles.

3. Blow a balloon up until it bursts.

4. Select a married female contestant to shave her husband with a plastic spoon. Be sure to protect his clothing with a shower curtain, sheet, or raincoat. Blindfold her; instruct her to put on the shaving cream, shave him with a plastic spoon, clean his face with a damp cloth, and put on after-shave lotion.

5. Blindfold two contestants, seat them facing each other, and give each a banana. Have them peel and then feed each other the bananas.

6. Give two contestants raincoats and water pistols filled with water. Give each a lighted candle. Each is to try to put out the other's candle with the water pistol.

7. Have one or more contestants sing one of these suggested songs:

"Row, Row, Row Your Boat"

"I've Been Working on the Railroad"

"Shine on Harvest Moon"

"Bicycle Built for Two"

8. Have a person pantomime (act without speaking) a person washing an elephant.

9. Two contestants share this consequence. Have one act as the straight man and the other sit on the first person's knee as the dummy. They must talk with each other unrehearsed. The straight man is to ask questions, the dummy is to answer. Allow about three minutes.

10. Play a recording of a symphony or a nursery rhyme and have the contestant conduct it as a famous conductor would. Supply the contestant with a baton.

Do not expect to ask all the questions or to complete all the consequences listed. A fellowship should last about thirty minutes, with time for refreshments and conversation.

Refreshments—Hot biscuits or rolls with butter; a variety of jellies and jams; coffee, milk, or hot chocolate.

Adapted from Bob and Carolyn Sessoms, *52 Complete Recreation Programs for Senior Adults* (Nashville: Convention Press, 1979), pp. 66-68. Used by permission.

SPOOKTACULAR

Arrange with a local funeral home for the use of a hearse or van bearing the name of their funeral service.

Prearrange with a local city or church cemetery to bring a group there on the night of the party. Be sure to get permission so as not to offend anyone who has loved ones buried there.

Have the group ride in the vehicle furnished by the funeral home, with cars following if needed. Take the group quietly to a predetermined area. After all have gathered, someone dressed in white, looking like a corpse and holding a lantern, rises from behind a tombstone and proceeds to read Edgar Allan Poe's "Tell-Tale Heart." As the story progresses, the group can hear the heart beating as someone behind another tombstone slowly beats on a box or bass drum. Nearby, another person is placed to operate the "beating heart." To do this, cut a large heart-shaped piece from a cardboard box and cover the hole with red crepe paper. Shine a flashlight on and off in the box as the heart beats. It gives a chilling effect.

Refreshments—Jelly-filled donuts and hot chocolate.

5

FUN WITH SEASONAL CELEBRATIONS

A FETE OF MONTHS

Arrange twelve tables or booths to represent the twelve months, with attendants in appropriate costume. Set up contests of various kinds at the booths. Suggestions for decorations:

January: Cotton-batting icicles. Falling snow represented by small balls of cotton tied to thread. Table with snow mound. Sled on top. Figure of Father Time, if obtainable. Attendants dressed in costumes trimmed with imitation ermine (cover cotton batting with mosquito netting and stripe with black ink or paint). Tiny calendar souvenirs.

February: Valentine decorations. White dresses trimmed with hearts. Candy heart souvenirs.

March: Green decorations. Girl and boy in Irish costumes. Shamrock souvenirs.

April: Rainbow colors. These colors fall about a large umbrella. Tiny umbrella souvenirs.

May: Maypole. Pink and green streamers from chandelier, ends held by tiny dolls at edges of table. Attendants in party dresses, wearing garlands about their heads. Daisies for souvenirs.

June: A rose booth, or table, with bride and groom as central figures. Large white wedding bell. Attendants in graduation dress. Roses for souvenirs.

July: Patriotic decorations. Uncle Sam and Miss Columbia in charge. Tiny flags for souvenirs.

August: Beach scene. Some sand, a large mirror or piece of glass for water, some tiny plastic dolls, etc. An amusing effect can be achieved by cutting some of the dolls in two. Some of them will then appear to be diving and others to be standing waist deep in water. Attendants in tennis costumes. Miniature fans for souvenirs.

September: Toy cardboard schoolhouse. Make miniature walk and fence. Tiny dolls carrying imitation books and slates. Attendants dressed as school "marms," or boy and girl dressed as school children. Souvenirs, small books, each with a riddle inside.

October: Halloween. Attendants in Halloween costume. Souvenirs, black cat cut-outs.

November: Fall leaves, turkey, horn-of-plenty. Or a football field with dolls or peanuts representing the players. Attendants, football player in uniform and cheerleader wearing sweater and carrying pennant. Small footballs or turkeys for souvenirs.

December: Green and red color scheme. Christmas bells, holly, etc. Santa Claus in charge. Christmas bells for souvenirs.

These suggestions for decorations can be used in many of the following parties.

JANUARY

A "BIG TIME" PARTY

Invitations—Invitations may be cut from cardboard in the form of little grandfather clocks. On the long narrow part of the clock, write this verse:

> Eve had no wrist watch,
> No watch had Adam;
> Didn't have a timepiece;
> Nobody had 'em.
> Nobody had a Big Time,
> You'd better believe;
> But you can have a Big Time
> On New Year's Eve—
> If you come to our Big Time Party.

Program—When the crowd arrives have them sing this song to the tune of "Smiles."

> There are Times that make us happy,
> There are Times that make us blue,
> There are Times that tend to make us snappy
> As alarm clocks mostly always do.
> There is Standard Time, and Daylight Saving;
> And, Old Timers, there's another, too.
> Do we hear you asking what that time is?
> It's the Big Time we're giving you.

Timely Tots: To insure that the party gets off to a hilarious start, dress each guest, regardless of sex, size, or protest, in a baby bonnet made of crepe paper. Prepare the bonnets beforehand and let several help you put them on.

What Time Is It? Now give each man a chance to get in the spotlight and show off his new bonnet. Have each one draw from a hat a slip of paper on which is written a word or phrase having to do with time. No two slips should be alike. The girls draw duplicate slips from another hat. Each man in turn steps forward and demonstrates his particular kind of time. His only chance of getting out of the spotlight is to act so effectively that the girl with a similar slip will recognize him as her partner. Guests are not allowed to show their slips. Slips should have phrases that are easily acted: killing time, marking time, beating time, losing time, timepiece.

Time to Sing: An impromptu singing contest is always fun. Select two leaders and let each choose singers for a choir. Give them five minutes to compose a suitable song, then have them sing the song, with actions.

Big Time Riddles: Each couple is supplied with one pencil and one sealed envelope containing a set of riddles. On the signal, all the envelopes are torn open and partners attack their riddles. Suggestions:

1. What makes a striking present? (clock)
2. When is a clock dangerous? (when it strikes one)
3. What day of the year is a command to go forward? (March 4th)
4. When the clock strikes 13, what time is it? (time to have it repaired)
5. What is always behind time? (back of the clock)
6. I have hands but no fingers, no bed but lots of ticks. What am I? (clock)
7. What is time and yet a fruit? (date)
8. What does the proverb say time is? (money)

Set an alarm clock to ring when time is up.

Refreshments—Chips, dips, snacks, and cold drinks.

A FATHER TIME PARTY

Invitations

Father Time would like to meet you,
In fact, he'd like to greet you

At a party giv'n in honor of his name.
There'll be fun a-bubbling over,
And you sure will be in clover;
If you miss it you will have yourself to blame.

Program

Father Time: Give players two minutes to see how many words they can make out of the letters in Father Time.

Baby Days
1. Milk drinking contest, using baby bottles.
2. Baby Show. Dress some of the crowd in baby caps. Have a committee judge the babies after putting them through various tests: weighing, using a piece of elastic under the shoulders; a bawling contest; test for beauty with the judges offering humorous criticisms.

Childhood Days: Play some children's game: London Bridge; Duck, Duck, Goose; or Drop the Handkerchief.

School Days
1. Everyone sing "School Days."
2. A spelling bee or living alphabet.
3. Anagrams.

Sweetheart Days
1. Draw for partners. Suspend a paper clockface in a doorway or from a chandelier. Through a hole in the center, strings drop down on either side. Boys hold the strings on one side and the girls hold the strings on the other. At a signal, they pull the strings and partners will be found holding the same string.
2. Partners work together on a contest. The answers have to do with watches or clocks.

Used before (second hand)
Seen at the circus (ring)
Fifteenth wedding anniversary (crystal)
What we give new members (h-our hand)

Women love them for adornment (jewels)
A watering place (springs)
The palmist looks them over (hands)
Read by the secretary (minutes)
Supports a flower (stem)
Sometimes, they claim, it stops a clock (face)
A tight-rope walker is good at it; and part of a bicycle (balance wheel)

Parent Days: Doll Dressing Contest. Each boy is required to dress a clothespin, plastic spoon, or peanut as a doll. Crepe paper, tape, glue, and colored pens or crayons are furnished. Each girl supervises the work of her partner.

Granddad Days: Rocking-chair Relay. The crowd is divided into two sides. From five to ten players are selected from each side, if crowd is large. Each contestant must run in bent-over position, holding the right hand on the back, to a rocking chair at the other side of the room, sit down, rock back and forth ten times, return to the starting line, and touch off the next teammate.

Refreshments—Brownies* topped with ice cream, beverage.

A PROPHECY PARTY

Prophecy Exchanges: Girls in outer circle, boys in inner. They march in opposite directions to music. When the music stops, players stop and face partners. Each one is given from fifteen to thirty seconds to tell the partner's future. In an exchange of experiences during the evening, it may be discovered that several boys have told each girl the same story.

Prophecy Web: A web is made of strings at one side of the room. Each player takes a loose end and begins to unravel the web, following the string to the end. It is tangled with other strings on the floor, and the player must stop to untangle the strings. This makes a good mixer. The strings are wound around chair and table legs and may go up and down stairs.

When the player comes to the end there is some sort of prophecy attached to the string. This may be accompanied by a trinket—a toy hammer, a horn, or a doll. With the hammer there would be a prophecy after this fashion: "A builder you will be. That's very plain to see." With the horn, there would be something like this: "In the orchestra you will play. At least it surely seems that way."

Ten Years from Now: One person goes around and whispers to each player the name of a place. Another gives them the name of a person. A third person tells them something they will be doing ten years from now. All players must then repeat what has been told them.

Fortunetelling: Introduce numerous fortunetelling devices.

1. Gypsy Fortuneteller. Booth with palmist.

2. Invisible Ink Fortunes. Write with lemon juice and hold over lighted candle to bring out the message.

3. Candle Fortune. Place six candles in a row. Label each with some prophecy of what is in store—misfortune, fortune, trip, a new friend, happiness, loss. The player is blindfolded, turned around, and given a chance to blow. The candle blown out indicates some future fate.

4. Fortunes from Cards.

Refreshments—Heavenly Hash*, beverage.

EVERYBODY'S BIRTHDAY PARTY

It is suggested that this social activity take place during the month of January, to celebrate everyone's birthday— for the coming year. Everyone should bring a white elephant gift wrapped for the festive occasion.

As guests arrive with their gifts, the leader ties a long string to each one. Later the gift table will be covered and the strings will hang out below the tablecloth. These will be used when the gifts are opened. Be sure to have extra gifts available in case someone forgets to bring one.

Decorations—Have twelve tables—one for each month. Each table should contain materials for decorating according to the various months: red and green—December; black and orange—October; green and white—March (St. Patrick's Day); red, white, and blue—July; etc. See A Fete of Months for more suggestions.

Crepe-paper streamers, posterboard, felt-tip pens, masking tape, thumbtacks, butcher paper or newsprint, scissors, and colored construction paper should be provided.

Let each guest go to the table of his or her birth month and begin to decorate the table. As other guests arrive, they join in. After all the tables have been decorated, let each group make up an original poem or song about their month. Ask the groups to share their compositions. For an additional activity, make name tags from leftover decorations.

Program—Begin by singing "Happy Birthday":

> Happy Birthday to you;
> Happy Birthday to me;
> Happy Birthday to all of us
> Happy Birthday to we.

Predicament/Solution: Hand each player a pencil and two pieces of paper. On one paper have each player write the question: "What would you do if . . . ?" and complete the predicament question. On the other piece of paper, each player writes the solution to that predicament. Pass the predicament question to the person on the left and the solution to the person on the right. Each person should have a predicament and a solution. Ask players to read the predicaments and the solutions they now have. The results should prove humorous.

Birthday Jewel: Since this is a birthday celebration, see how many can guess the answers in this paper and pencil activity. Match the month with the appropriate birthstone by placing the correct letter beside the number:

_____	1.	January	a. Emerald
_____	2.	February	b. Peridot
_____	3.	March	c. Diamond
_____	4.	April	d. Garnet
_____	5.	May	e. Turquoise
_____	6.	June	f. Opal
_____	7.	July	g. Amethyst
_____	8.	August	h. Pearl
_____	9.	September	i. Ruby
_____	10.	October	j. Topaz
_____	11.	November	k. Sapphire
_____	12.	December	l. Aquamarine

Answers: (1) d; (2) g; (3) l; (4) c; (5) a; (6) h; (7) i; (8) b; (9) k; (10) f; (11) j; (12) e.

Open the Presents: Seat everyone in a circle. Let the person whose next birthday is farthest in the future go to the gift table, take a string, pull out a gift, open it, and show it to everybody. Then the other guests, one by one, choose and open gifts. The person whose birthday is today or closest to today may choose the last gift or select one that has already been opened. If that person takes someone else's gift, be sure the remaining gift is presented to the person whose gift was taken.

Share a Birthday: Have guests return to their tables. Ask each person to relate to the others at the table the most meaningful birthday he or she remembers. After everyone shares, ask someone from each table to share a birthday experience with the whole group.

Refreshments—If lunch or dinner is a part of the party, either have everyone bring a covered dish, or have the meal prepared. Chicken Casserole* or Lasagna* would be good choices. Be sure to have cake and ice cream.

Adapted from Bob and Carolyn Sessoms, *52 Complete Recreation Programs for Senior Adults* (Nashville: Convention Press, 1979), pp. 48-49. Used by permission.

COUPLES' PARTY

For a New Year's Eve get-together, invite several couples. After having an opportunity to just socialize, ask the women to sit on one side of the room and the men on the opposite side to play this game. Husbands and wives should sit directly across from one another. Give each person pencil and paper. As you ask the questions, direct some to women only and some to men only. However, everyone is to answer all the questions—husbands and wives answer the way they think their mates will respond.

Suggestions for questions to ask the husbands:

1. What is your wife's favorite color?
2. Where did you take your wife on your first date?
3. On what day of the week were you married?
4. What was your wife wearing when you first met?
5. If your wife could have lunch with any movie actor, who would it be?
6. Which of the following would best describe your wife: cream puff, pretzel, prune?
7. What color is your wife's toothbrush?
8. How many windows are in your house?
9. What was the name of the last movie you saw with your wife?
10. What is your wife's favorite leisure-time activity?

11. Would you describe your wife as being more like Miss Piggy, Twiggy, or Wonder Woman?

12. What is the one thing you would like to change about your wife?

13. What is your wife's greatest asset?

Questions to ask the wives:

1. Would your neighbors describe your marriage as "Good Times," "Family Feud," or "Love Boat"?

2. What would you like to change about your husband?

3. What year model was your first family car?

4. What was the first gift you received from your husband?

5. What is your husband's favorite leisure-time activity?

6. Does the kitchen sink face north, south, east, or west?

7. Which of the following would best describe your husband: Superman, Scrooge, Casanova, or Lone Ranger?

8. If you could keep only one thing in your house, what would it be?

9. If you had a choice for a second honeymoon, where would you go?

10. What is your husband's favorite dessert?

11. If your husband could be stranded on a deserted island with one of the following, which would it be: Raquel Welch, Goldie Hawn, or Dolly Parton?

12. What was the name of your husband's last girlfriend before he met you?

13. Name a song that was sung at your wedding.

Have couples compare their answers. Give a prize to the couple having the most matching answers.

FEBRUARY

CUPID'S CARNIVAL OF HEARTS

Publicity

Come one, come all, to the
prodigiously produced
and picturesquely presented

CARNIVAL OF HEARTS

Friday, February 14
8 o'clock

———

Innumerable Innovations

———

Notable Novelties

———

A Full Evening of Fun,
Frolic, and Fellowship

———

Decorations—Booths, which can be made by fastening thin posts to the front legs of tables, are placed around the room and appropriately decorated with hearts, cupids, and red and white crepe paper.

Program—Each guest on arrival is given a small tally card on which to keep score. The person having the highest score at the end of the evening is given some suitable prize.

Sticker Mixer: Have small hearts (about two inches in diameter) prepared with various words printed on them— Love, Honeymoon, Courtship, Marriage, Acquaintance, etc. These are placed on the backs of the guests. The object of the game is for the guests to find out, by asking questions, what word is on their card. When they succeed, they may remove their hearts and stick them on the backs of others.

When a sufficient number of people have arrived, the booths can be opened for business. The person in charge of each booth should have a spiel similar to that of those who conduct sideshow attractions.

Heart Darts: Cut a dartboard out of red cardboard in the shape of a heart, about two feet in diameter. On this mount small white hearts about four inches wide, with the following inscriptions: Single Blessedness; Acquaintance-ship; Friendship; Love; Courtship; Engagement; Marriage. In the center mount a black heart labeled Refusal. The board is erected about seven feet back of the stand.

Each player is given seven darts to try making the round of hearts up to Marriage without hitting the black heart. A person who succeeds the first time is given 25 points and continues to another booth. One who succeeds on the second try is awarded 10 points, and on the third try, 5 points are awarded. No person is allowed to try more than three times. As an additional prize at this and other booths small chocolate dolls can be given.

Fortunetelling Booth: A girl dressed to represent the Queen of Hearts is in charge of this booth. She reveals the fortunes of the guests, especially about love, marriage, etc.

Wheel of Fortune: A wheel is made of fiberboard and marked off in twelve sections—Journey, Success, True Love, Health, Happiness, Early Marriage, Wealth, etc. This is fastened on an upright post with an indicator at the top of the wheel. The wheel should have a small spool at the center and be mounted on a flat-headed nail. Those who spin the wheel and land on Matrimonial Bliss or Wealth get 25 points; those on True Love or Happiness, 10 points; Success or Early Marriage, 5 points.

Heart Toss: Make five heart-shaped rings of heavy wire. The hearts should be about four inches wide. Three upright sticks about a half-inch in diameter and six inches high are fastened on a board placed about six feet from the player. The sticks are labeled Happiness, Wealth, and Disappointment. Those who ring the sticks with three or more hearts receive 25 points. Two ringers earn a score of 10, and five points are given to anyone ringing one stick.

Cupid's Shooting Gallery: Purchase a toy bow and some arrows. Make a large heart of fiberboard and mark smaller hearts on it, similar to the rings on a target. Those hitting the center are given 25 points. The next circles count 15, 10, and 5 respectively.

Cupid's Fish Pond: Wrap a number of small metal novelties—thimble, wedding ring, engagement ring, coin, horn, button, etc., in red paper and tie them with string. Each contestant fishes for one article, using a stick and string with a bent pin. In addition to receiving the article indicating a fortune, the player is given 25 points for securing a wedding ring, 10 points for an engagement ring, and 5 points for a coin.

Heart Race: Cut four red hearts out of heavy cardboard. These should be about fifteen inches in diameter. The group is divided into two equal teams for a relay race. Each team is given two hearts. Contestants must lay the hearts down and step from one to the other, racing to a given point and back. Each member of the winning team receives 25 points. The losers each receive 10 points.

Midway Attraction: Divide the crowd into two or three groups and give each group ten minutes to prepare some stunt around the theme, "How a modern man and maid became engaged."

Refreshments—This booth is closed until most of the evening's program has been completed. Serve heart-shaped cookies with red and white icing and punch or pink lemonade.

DAN CUPID'S HOSPITAL PARTY

Invitations—These could be written in the form of prescriptions and placed in pill bottles.

Dan Cupid, M.D., is opening an office at ___

Hours: 8-10:30 P.M.   Date _____

Program—A doctor and nurse in charge examine guests as they enter. Each person is assigned to one of the following wards in the hospital.

Broken-hearted............................Accident Ward
Aching hearts...........................Operating Room
Misplaced hearts.............................Sanitarium
Lost hearts............................Emergency Ward
Tender Hearts..........................Children's Ward

If there is a large crowd, divide into five groups as indicated and start each group of guests in its particular ward. They then progress to the other wards in order, until they have visited every ward. Prizes may be awarded to those scoring the most points and to the group with the highest scores.

Accident Ward: Give each person a large heart cut into many pieces. Tape is provided. The first person to mend a heart will receive five points. All others who finish before the group has to move on will receive two points.

Operating Ward: Scissors and paper are given each person. The one who cuts out the largest number of hearts (well shaped) in two minutes will receive five points. All players who make at least ten hearts will receive two points.

Heart's Ease Sanitarium: Place a wastebasket on the floor. Players are given twenty-five cardboard hearts to toss. Score five points for the winner and two points for each person who gets as many as five cards in the wastebasket. Players stand or sit at a distance of five or six feet.

Emergency Ward: Have guests make as many words as possible from the letters in the words Lost Hearts. Five points to the winner and two points to each person making as many as ten words.

Children's Ward: Make three wire hearts and cover the wire with crepe paper. Suspend them from a chandelier or doorway. Above each is a jingle:

> Blow your bubble through Number One
> And you'll be married and have a son.

> To be engaged within the week,
> Number Two is the one you seek.

> An awful fate for Number Three—
> A spinster or bachelor you will be.

Guests are provided with a bubble pipe, fan, and bubble solution. The bubble must be thrown off the pipe and then blown through a heart by means of the fan. Players are given ten tries to get a bubble through one of the hearts. Two points are awarded for success.

Convalescent Ward: All guests are now invited into the convalescent ward where progressive table games are played.

Refreshments—Banana-split Cake* and lemonade or Lime Punch*.

A VALENTINE PARTY

Invitations—On hearts about four inches wide, write the following invitation:

Merry hearts, dearest hearts,
Fun and frolic galore!
A Valentine Party we're having;
A hearty time in store.
(date and time)   (place)

For each place the word *heart* is used, paste a tiny red heart.

Decorations—Decorations will do much to make your party a success. Use festoons of red and white crepe paper. Strings of small red hearts cut from construction paper and draped about the walls or hanging from chandeliers are very effective.

Program

Mixer: As the guests enter, give each either a red or a white heart. On the back of each heart is written the name of a famous lover, the names of the men going to the boys, the names of the women, to the girls. Suggestions: Romeo and Juliet, Punch and Judy, Jack and Jill, the Prince and Cinderella, Priscilla and John Alden, Hiawatha and Minnehaha, Napoleon and Josephine, Jacob and Rachel, Ruth and Boaz, Prince Charles and Lady Diana, John F. Kennedy and Jackie Bouvier, etc. Of course, Romeo must find Juliet; Punch, Judy; and so on. If the crowd is large, or merely to make things more complicated, let there be a duplicate list of names on both red and white hearts. Then Romeo with a white heart must find the Juliet with a white heart; Romeo with a red heart must find Juliet with a red heart, etc. The couples with red hearts form one team, the couples with white hearts, another.

A Love Letter: The letters of the alphabet are written on small hearts. Each couple is given a large paper bag containing one complete alphabet. At the signal, the bags are opened and each player is allowed to draw two hearts at a time from the bag. The couple who first succeeds in drawing out the letters L O V E wins, and five points are scored for their group (Red or White).

A Honeymoon Trip: A large map of the world is fastened to the wall. Each couple selects the country they would like to visit on their honeymoon. They write the name of the place selected on tiny red hearts. Then they are blindfolded and, holding hands, must try to pin their hearts as near as possible on the place selected. The couple pinning the hearts closest to the proposed destination gains five points for their group.

Lost Arrows: Small red and white arrows are hidden about the room. On each arrow is written one of the following words: Love, Friendship, Acquaintance, Deceit, Jealousy. The red arrows must duplicate the white arrows exactly. Captains are elected for each group. At a given signal, the hunt for lost arrows is started. Members of the Red team collect only red arrows and members of the White team collect only white arrows. At the end of three minutes the hunt is stopped, and captains collect and count their arrows. The arrows score as follows: For each arrow marked Love, five points; for Friendship, three; Acquaintance, one; for each marked Deceit, subtract five points; for Jealousy, subtract three. The winning side scores ten points.

Heart and Dart Contest: Cut a large red heart from heavy cardboard. From this heart cut out three small hearts, each a different size. Above the smallest opening, mark "15"; above the next larger, "10"; and above the largest, "5." Suspend the large heart in a doorway. With a dart made of a red feather and a needle stuck in a large cork, each contestant is allowed three throws at the heart. Players' scores are added to their groups' scores, and the winning group at the end of the contest is awarded 10 points.

Making Valentines: Chairs are arranged in a row alternately, one facing one way, the next the other. There are as many chairs as players, excepting the Valentine Maker. Each player is given the name of some material or tool used in valentine making. (Hearts, arrows, cupids, colored papers, scissors, paste, rhymes, crayons, etc.) There may be several with the same name. The Valentine Maker starts marching around the chairs, calling for the materials needed to make a valentine. As their names are called, the players must rise and follow. When there are enough, the Valentine Maker calls "Posted," and everyone makes a jump for a chair. The one left standing is now the Valentine Maker and continues the game.

Building a Love Nest: This is a drawing relay race. A chalkboard is divided into two equal spaces, one for the Reds and one for the Whites. The contestants of each group should line up, one behind the other, facing the space of board allotted them. Each captain is told to draw the outline of a house; the second member of each team is to draw the roof; the third, the chimney; the fourth, the windows and door; the fifth, the sidewalks; the sixth, the flowers in the yard, etc., until each has a definite part assigned in building the love nest. A piece of chalk is given each captain, the signal given, and the fun begins. The group that first succeeds in completing a recognizable Love Nest is the winner of five points. It would add to the interest to provide each side with colored chalk. If desired, the winner may be decided on the basis of the most artistic creation.

Cupid's Heart Exchange: Players sit in a circle. Each has the name of one of four kinds of hearts—Merry Heart, Contented Heart, Happy Heart, Broken Heart. One player stands in the center and, as Cupid, does the bargaining. Pointing to a certain player in the circle, Cupid says, "I want your heart." This player asks, "What will you give in exchange?" Cupid must answer with one of the four kinds of hearts. If the player says, "I'll take it," then that player and all the other players bearing the name of the heart mentioned must change places. In the mixup, Cupid seeks to secure a chair. If, however, the player does not wish to accept the bargain, the player says, "Wait until Leap Year!" and everyone must change places. Of course, whoever fails to secure a chair is Cupid and must start the bargaining again.

At the end of the games, points are totaled and the winning group awarded a box of candy hearts, or allowed to be seated and be served refreshments by members of the losing group.

Refreshments—Vanilla ice cream with tiny red candy hearts sprinkled over the top; heart-shaped cookies or Strawberry Layer Cake* decorated with hearts.

—CLYDE KENNEDY

VALENTINE PARTY GAMES

Guess What? Meet guests as they arrive and on the back of each, pin a heart with a word appropriate to the season—Honeymoon, Courtship, Marriage, Rice, Bride, Groom. The guests are then required to guess their labels by the conversation addressed to them by other guests. "Was it a happy one?" "Where did you go?" "How long have you been back?" are questions that might be shot at the girl with Honeymoon on her back.

Make a Valentine: Furnish guests with red and white paper, scissors, colored magazine pictures, paste, tape, and scraps of lace paper. Let each one make a fancy valentine. Send these to shut-ins and to hospitals.

Hunting Hearts: Hearts of different colors are hidden about the room. Some are numbered and some are not. At a signal, players hunt for the hearts. When all hearts are found, players are privileged to trade for colors and numbers they think may be valuable. The values are unknown to the players until the trading is over. The leader then announces the values, and players add up their scores.

Each white heart...1 point
7 hearts adds 50 points to the score
Each green heart...5 points
11 doubles the score
Each blue heart..2 points
13 subtracts 20 from the score
Each red heart..10 points
15 adds 75 points

Valentine Fashions: Provide materials for a Valentine fashion show—yards of crepe paper in various bright colors, some newspapers, paper lace (perhaps cut out of newspapers), tape, scissors, pins, and ornaments of all sorts. Have each girl dress a man in becoming Valentine costume, or divide into small groups and have each group dress one person. Have a parade of the models.

Marooned: Men form a circle in one end of the room and women form another at the opposite end. A large paper heart is placed inside each circle. Players march to music. When the music stops all players stop, and the man and woman on or nearest the bottom point of the heart in each circle are taken out to become partners for the next game. This continues until all players have partners.

Progressive Fortune: Give each player paper and pencil. Tell players to write their own name at the top, fold it under, and pass the paper to the right. Players now write some future date and someone's name. Again the paper is folded and passed on. Then they write what will happen; then the name of a place; then something a person possesses; then how it was gotten; then the effect it has. When each paper is unfolded, it tells a strange story. It might sound like this: "Earl Jones and May Martin on

July 4, 1990, played the piano in Chicago. They had jewelry which they got by main force and awkwardness. They lived happily ever after."

Where's Your Heart? Players sit in a circle. The first one turns to the right-hand neighbor and says, "Where's your heart?" The neighbor gives any reply, such as, "My heart is in a sycamore tree." The questioner must now respond with something that rhymes with "tree"—perhaps, "Well, that's good enough for me." So it goes all around the circle. Any player who cannot respond with a rhyme might be required to perform some stunt.

Heart Snatch: Players form a circle and march to music. On chairs against the walls are paper hearts, one to each chair. There is one chair less than the number of players. When the music stops all players rush to sit in a chair, first picking up the heart. If two players arrive at the same time, the one who gets the heart is the one who stays in the game. The player who fails to get a heart drops out of the game and sits on one of the chairs when the marching resumes, thus eliminating one chair. This continues until only one player is left.

Eternal Triangle: Divide players into two sides facing one another. On each count, each side has decided whether it shall represent the coy maiden, the lover, or the preacher. The coy maiden is represented by assuming coy expression with finger under the chin. The lover holds one hand over the heart and extends the other hand beseechingly. The preacher stands with upraised hands in blessing. The maiden beats the lover; lover beats the preacher; and preacher beats the maiden. The whole side must do the same action. The leader will count three and immediately, all members of both sides must assume the character they have decided upon. The first side to score three points is winner.

Progressive Conversation: Each player signs up for one topic. One minute is given for each subject. The following topics are suggested: 1. My First Date. 2. Why Marry? 3. Qualifications for a Good Mother-in-law. 4. The Best Way to Propose. 5. Shall the Preacher Kiss the Bride?

Valentine Jigsaw Puzzle: Paste valentines on pieces of stiff cardboard. Cut in a number of pieces. Be sure to keep each valentine in a separate envelope. Have each person or group put a valentine jigsaw puzzle together. Provide tape.

MARCH

A MARCH WIND PARTY

Invitations

> Blow around to _____,
> Friday evening, March ___, and enjoy the
> March Wind Party. Bring along your raincoat.

Decorations—When guests arrive have electric fans blowing streamers of crepe or tissue paper from the sides of the room. Have the room decorated with toy balloons, green paper, and serpentine streamers. Place placards about the room with such messages as the following:

Blow yourself to a good time tonight.
What city is known as The Windy City?
Blow about your achievements as much as you like, but don't burst your bellows.
Don't try to blow out the electric light.
Blow your own horn, if you want it blown.
Heard from a Flat Tire: "Some blow-out."
Obituary: "A sad tale, alas—He blew out the gas."

Program

Visit to Cave-of-the-Winds: All who wish to enter the cave are asked to don their raincoats. A guide then conducts guests through a dark passageway, after asking them to take hold of a rope which the guide holds. This, it is explained, is necessary in order that none might be lost.

At one place in the dark passageway, someone is stationed with an atomizer and a fan. The atomizer is filled with clear water and is sprayed on the visitors to the cave. Following the spray, a swoop of the fan adds to the peculiar sensation.

Entering a room that is fitted up as the Cave-of-the-Winds, the visitors are introduced to King Wind. This person has a long white beard and wears a flowing robe and a crown. Speaking through a megaphone, he welcomes the guests.

"Welcome to my Kingdom, children of the earth. Welcome, thrice welcome.

> I blow from the West,
> I blow from the East,
> From the North and South,
> On man and on beast.

"Let me introduce you to my assistants, the Four Winds of the Earth."

Immediately there step forth four attendants in long flowing robes. Each holds a long horn and on the command of the King, "Blow ye Four Winds of the Earth!" they blow lustily. When they do, the air is filled with a white mist and those visitors in front find themselves covered with white flour. If desired, the horns may be loaded with confetti, instead. The guide then leads the visitors from the cave.

If not possible to take all the people on this tour at one time, divide them into two parties, swearing the first to secrecy.

The cave should be very dimly lighted, and fans should furnish a breezy atmosphere. A vacuum cleaner might be rigged up to blow out instead of in, to furnish occasional gusts of wind.

Blowing Contest: Divide the crowd into two groups. Blindfold the players one at a time and give each three tries to blow out a lighted candle. Count a point each time the candle is blown out. The side with the best score wins.

A Breezy Race: Four to ten players represent each side. Furnish each player with a cardboard fan and ten tiny tissue-paper balls, one color for each side. At the signal, all players start fanning their tissue-paper balls to the goal at the opposite side of the room. Two large boxes several feet apart are placed so that the balls may be fanned into them. No player is allowed to scrape the ball in; fans must blow them along. At the end of one minute the side with the largest number of balls in its respective goal wins. No player may blow a ball into the opponent's goal.

Feather Blow
1. Fill jars with downy feathers, one jar for each contestant. The first who is able to blow all feathers out of the jar wins.
2. Furnish one downy feather to each contestant. Two players compete at a time, one from each side. At the signal, players throw their feathers into the air and start blowing them toward a goal line. Ten points are scored for crossing the goal line. Ten points are awarded the opponent each time a feather falls to the floor. When a feather does fall, it must be picked up at the point where it fell and started again, after the contestant has taken three long steps backward.

Windy Words: Each side is given one minute to write down all the words relating to winds that players can recall. One player in each group should write down words as they are suggested. Suggestions: breeze, gust, gale, blast, roar, cyclone, tornado, squall, whiff, puff, etc.

Refreshments—Ice-cream sundaes with toppings.

A SPRING PARTY

Invitations

> The flowers that bloom in the spring, Tra-la,
> Have nothing to do with the case;
> But at our Spring Party you'll laugh a ha-ha,
> So bring your smilingest face.

Decorations—Flowers, green and white crepe paper.

Program

Spring a Joke: Provide a number of magazines with joke pages. Let each person look up a good joke to spring on the crowd. Try to have one joke page for each guest.

Or clip jokes out of magazines and let each guest draw one from a box.

Or pin the jokes on each person. Then form concentric circles and march the boys in one direction and the girls in the other. When the music stops, they stop and face one another, and each person reads another's joke. This might serve as a good mixer for a large crowd.

Spring a Spring Poem: Give each guest an unfinished spring rhyme to which the last line must be added. For a large crowd, divide into groups and give each group a poem. Suggestions:

> Spring is the season of the year
> That some folk seem to hold most dear.
> It looks so gay in color green,
>
> _____.

> The rose still blushes and the violets blow,
> The spinach still "spins" and the onions grow,
> The lettuce still "lets" and the turnips "turn,"
>
> _____.

When daisies pied, and violets blue,
And Lady-smocks all silver-white,
And cuckoo-buds of yellow hue,

_____ .

Many players can receive the same poem.
Variation: Let guests repeat poems they have memorized.

Spring a Spring Bonnet: Provide newspapers, crepe paper, scissors, tape, pins, paste, and pictures of ladies' hats. Let each guest make a hat to wear for a while, at least. An award may be given for the best spring bonnet.
Variation: Divide the crowd into groups and have each group make one or two models to be worn by persons selected from their group.

Spring a Song: Write the names of songs on slips of paper. There should be at least four slips for each song. Have the players draw the slips from a box. Then each player looks for the rest of the quartet. As they find one another they link arms. Each quartet must sing its song. Then all the quartets may be required to perform simultaneously, each singing its own song.

Spring a Stunt: Divide into two or more groups and have each group present some stunt. The general theme could be Signs of Spring. Suggestions: In the Spring a Young Man's Fancy; Mr. Jones' Vegetable Garden; House-cleaning Days; Spring Fever.

Refreshments—Banana Torte* and Shirley Temple Punch*.

AN IRISH PARTY

March 17 is St. Patrick's Day. Patrick is said to have brought Christianity to Ireland about A.D. 450. Legends say he drove the snakes out of Ireland, brought darkness upon his enemies, and performed many miracles. Why not make your March party a St. Patrick's Day party?

Invitations—A shamrock, cut from either white or green cardboard, may bear these words written in green ink, in limerick fashion:

> Shure, won't you come to our party?
> You'll find a welcome that's hearty.
> Come Friday e'en,
> Wearin' some green,
> An Irish joke bring to our party.
> *(date and time)*   *(place)*

Decorations—Shamrocks cut from green paper, jonquils or other spring flowers, green candles in candleholders made from potatoes by carving out a place for the candle.

Program

Irish Family Assignments: Divide the crowd into groups of ten each. Let each group be an Irish "family." Each member of a family may be given an Irish first name also. Suggested family names: Murphy, Mulligan, O'Shea, Maloney, O'Flaherty, Flannigan, O'Reilly, Kelly, O'Grady, Casey. The members of one family, for example, might be Ma, Pa, Pat, Mike, Bridget, Judy, Jo, Kathleen, Jerry, and Rosie. When the guests enter, each one is given a slip of paper tied with a bit of green ribbon, on which is written a complete Irish name. Example: Jerry Murphy. While the crowd is assembling, early comers will enjoy discovering the other members of their "families."

The Lakes of Killarney: For this game a rough outline map of lakes should be drawn on the floor with chalk. Music is played while the crowd marches in and out and around the room. When the music stops, anyone standing in a "lake" must drop out of the game. The lakes should be

drawn close together. This game may be played until all
but a few persons have had to drop out.

Irish Family Reunions: Announcement is made that
there are certain Irish families that are holding reunions
tonight. Each family is asked to get together for group
games.

1. Joke Contest. Each member of the family is asked to
tell an Irish joke. The family decides which joke is best.
Later in the evening, the entire group will hear a
representative from each family tell the Irish joke
considered best.

2. Limericks. Limericks are nonsense poems said to
have originated in Ireland and to have received their name
from the city of Limerick on the banks of the river
Shannon. Limericks are read to the entire crowd and
limerick structure explained.

An often-quoted limerick:

> There was a young lady of Niger,
> Who smiled as she rode on a tiger,
> They returned from the ride
> With the lady inside,
> And the smile on the face of the tiger.

A limerick consists of five lines. Lines 1, 2, and 5 contain
three poetic "feet" and rhyme; lines 3 and 4 contain two
feet and rhyme. Each family is given the first line and
asked to complete the limerick. Each family will recite its
limerick as a group. Suggested first lines:

> There was an old man in a tree.
> There was an old man in a boat.
> There was a typist so pretty.
> There was a young maiden of Dallas.
> A flapper down in Atlanta.
> There was a young man from Mobile.
> An aviator flew in the sky.
> There was a small boy who went fishin'.
> Susie went to a movie show.
> An old maid with a permanent wave.

3. Irish stunts. Each family is asked to plan an impromptu Irish stunt. Give not more than five minutes to get the stunts ready. They may then be given before the entire crowd by the families in turn. Charades, using the names of Irish towns or words, may be substituted for the stunts.

Securing Partners for Refreshments: Cut two of one size of the following objects out of green cardboard: shamrock, rose, pipe, snake, pig, Irish harp. By varying the size or shape, enough different objects may be made for your groups. The girls draw objects from one tray, the boys from another. Objects are then matched for partners for refreshments.

Refreshments—Either potato salad or a green gelatin salad; sandwiches made of bread cut in the shape of a shamrock; green mints; Lime Punch*.

APRIL

April Fool—Around the world April Fool, or what corresponds to it, is observed. A brief poem reveals that this celebration is of ancient origin.

> The first of April some do say
> Is set apart as All Fool's Day;
> But why people call it so
> Nor I nor they themselves do know.

In some ancient countries it was regarded with superstition. No one would dare plan an enterprise, and only the very brave or foolhardy would venture to marry on that day. Napoleon married Maria Louisa on April 1, 1810, but the superstitious would point to him as Exhibit A.

The French call it *poisson d'avril*—"April Fish." The inference is that they're easily caught. There is a French story of a woman who stole a gold watch from the home of a friend. When, after a lively chase, the police caught her, she cried, "Poisson d'avril." But the judge had a sense of humor also, and he sentenced her to jail until the next All Fool's Day.

In various countries all sorts of hoaxes are played on this day. It is the day for practical jokes. Neighbors and friends are sent on fool's errands. Companions are tricked into doing foolish things.

AN APRIL FOOL'S PARTY

A Fool Picture: The guests form a single line. They are told they are to see a wonderful picture. Have them go singly past a mirror marked with the words *April Fool* written in soap.

Fool Contest: Choose three or four guests to take part in this ten-second contest. They are to say, "What am I doing?" ten times in ten seconds. The crowd answers, "Making fools of yourselves."

False Alarm: The dinner gong will sound and someone will announce, "Dinner is not served."

Drawing the Moon: Form a circle. With a stick, draw an imaginary picture of the man in the moon, putting in the eyes, nose, and mouth. Pass the stick to the next person, saying, "Do this." The trick is not in drawing the face but in changing the stick from one hand to the other when passing it to the next person. Continue until each person solves the mystery.

Foolish Rhyming Contest: Each person is given pencil and paper. The paper has ten letters written on it. Everybody can receive the same ten letters, or each person can receive different letters. Guests must create words beginning with those ten letters and then compose a rhyming verse with the words. They do not need to use all ten letters. The best verses are read aloud. Examples:

A P R I L   F O O L S

A—apples—and—a	F—fruit
P—pear	O—only
R	O—oranges
I—I	L—lemons
L—like	S—share

Fruit only I share,
Like oranges, lemons, apples, and a pear.

April Fool Race: This game is the old favorite Obstacle Race. Select two contestants. Place a number of obstacles in the race course—upturned chairs, buckets, ropes tied from one side of the room to the other, etc. Let the contestants try the course first, walking through it with their eyes open. Then blindfold them and tell them they must make their way to the end of the course. In the meantime, someone has quietly removed all the obstacles. This race will provide lots of fun, especially if the contestants are not allowed to run and are told that every obstacle touched will count a point against them.

April Fool Conversation: A long string is required. Two players who know the trick hold the ends of the string and prepare to carry on a "telephone" conversation. All the players are told to hold the string between their teeth if they wish to hear a most interesting conversation. After a short humorous conversation between the players holding the ends of the string, one asks the other, "Where have you been?" The answer comes back, "I've been fishing." "Catch anything?" "Yes, here's a whole string of suckers."

April Fool Locomotion: This is simply the Kiddie Kar Relay that is always plenty of fun. Choose as the contestants for this race the tallest, fattest, or most awkward members of your group. Use from two to four on each of two teams. The first contestants are given Kiddie Kars and at the signal, sit down on them and without a push, start propelling their Kars toward the goal. If they get back, they give the Kar to the next member of their teams, who go through the same ordeal. Continue until one side wins.

April Shower Race: Several couples are needed for this race. They stand in line, with a closed suitcase and an umbrella in front of each couple. In each suitcase there are a pair of rubbers, a pair of gloves, a raincoat, and a hat. At the signal, each young man grabs his suitcase, and hand in hand, he and his partner rush to the opposite goal. When they arrive, he opens the suitcase, hands his partner the rubbers, which she puts on, then hands her each of the other articles, which she in turn puts on. He then closes the suitcase and raises the umbrella and, holding the umbrella over his partner with one hand and the suitcase in the other, runs with her back to the starting point. When they arrive, he must close the umbrella, open the suitcase, help his partner take off her "rainy day apparel," replace it in the suitcase, and close it.

An April Fool Tea Party: The use of this game in any form usually turns the thoughts of the players toward food, so it is well to use it near the close of the program. Players form a large circle. The one who begins this game is "on to the trick" and begins the game by saying, "My grandmother doesn't like tea, but she likes _____," inserting the name of some food or beverage that does not contain the letter T. Each player in turn repeats the sentence and inserts the name of some food. The fun comes in seeing who will be the first to catch on. Grandmother doesn't like tea; therefore she doesn't like anything with T in it.

Refreshments—Give each person a copy of the menu on the left below and tell guests to choose three items from the list.

Menu	*Item to Be Served*
Spring's offering	Water
New England brains	Boston baked beans
What we people need	Bread
First love	Candy kisses
Some calendar figures	Dates
Can't be beaten	Boiled egg
Honeymooners' prayer	Lettuce alone
A letter in the alphabet	Tea
Hidden tears	Onions
A chip off the old block	Toothpicks
Lover's greens	Pickles
Sweet sixteen	Sugar

After the orders have been filled according to the list on the right, the plates should be taken up and the "real" refreshments served. Sandwiches, tea and cookies, with perhaps a pickle, would be appropriate. Unpalatable April fool confections or food are not in good taste in more ways than one.

MUGGY AWARDS FELLOWSHIP

Any group—a group of friends, a school group, a fraternity, a club, or a church group can sponsor the Annual Muggy Awards. Pattern it after the Academy Awards or some other awards show.

Select a master of ceremonies with a good sense of humor. This person can either present all the awards or introduce others to present them. The Muggy can be just a paper cup or it can be a real mug. The categories are meant to be humorous. No award is to be derogatory or defaming

to any person. It is all in good fun. Some categories for
Muggy:

> Best Cook of the Year
> Biggest Eater of the Year
> Person Who Starts the Most Diets in a Year
> Best Singer (not really)
> Country-western Fan of the Year
> Football Widow Award
> Jogger of the Year
> Joker of the Year
> Secretary of the Year
> Nut of the Year
> Giver of the Year

Refreshments—After the awards, enjoy fruit-and-ginger-
ale punch made with lime ice cream; finger sandwiches.

MAY

AN OLD CLOTHES PARTY

Each person is expected to come wearing old clothes—
old overalls, torn jeans, ragged clothes.

As guests arrive, a patch bearing his or her name is
pinned on each person's back. This is to be worn
throughout the evening.

Dress-up Contest: This is similar to the old Honeymoon
Race idea. Several boxes contain hats, coats, etc. One box is
given to each couple. On the signal, each couple must open
the box and dress in the garments found there. They must
then run to a stated point, return, remove the garments,
and put them back in the box. The first couple to finish
wins. Where there is a large crowd, representatives may be
chosen for the two sides.

Clothespin Race: Have each side line up single file. Give the first person in each line two handfuls of clothespins. These are to be passed overhead, one at a time, till they reach the last person in line. That player then runs to the head of the line and starts the pins backward again. This continues until the original head player is back at that position. For each pin dropped, one point is scored to the opposition. The side that completes the round first is awarded three points.

Hanging Clothes: Five to ten players for each side line up single file at the starting point. The starting player has a clothespin and a towel or handkerchief. At the far side of the playing space, a clothesline has been strung. The first player must run to this clothesline and hang the towel or handkerchief with the clothespin. The second player in line must run and remove the pin and towel, bringing them back to player Number Three. So it continues until all the players have run the course.

Clothes Grab: An old rag is placed at a point midway between the two lines of players. The two lines of players number off. The leader calls a number and the two players having that number rush out to the center. One of them finally grabs the rag and is pursued back to his or her own line by the other. Two points are scored if the player returns to the line without being tagged. One point is scored for the opposition if the player with the rag is tagged.

Clothes Basket: Played like Fruit Basket. Players are numbered off by fours. The ones are "shoes," twos are "hats," threes are "coats," and fours are "vests." "Clothes basket upset!" means everyone changes seats.

Old Songs: Close the party by singing some of the old songs—"Silver Threads Among the Gold," "When You and I Were Young, Maggie," "Annie Laurie," "Long, Long Ago," "Old Folks at Home."

Refreshments—Wieners, buns, and condiments; soft drinks.

A TENNIS PARTY

At least one tennis court should be available. Set up tables for anagrams, checkers, chess, and other table games. Two to four persons will use the court for one to three games. The rest gather at the tables and play games.

Mixer: Strings are wound in and out through the meshes of the net across the court. There should be one string for each two persons. Players are told to take the end of a string and untangle it, the girls starting from one side and the boys from the other. When the string is untangled a boy and a girl will be holding it. These two are partners for refreshments or for some game.

Balloon Tennis: A large durable toy balloon can be the ball. Players use their hands as rackets. As many players can play as can get on the court. The ball is put in play by one player near the net batting it high in the air. Players may hit the ball as many times in succession as they desire. When the ball hits the ground the play is over. Score as in regular tennis.

Serving Blindfolded: Players are blindfolded, turned around, and attempt to serve. Any player getting the ball over the net scores a point. Or blindfolded players could toss the ball over the net.

Refreshments—Peanut Blossoms* and ice-cold lemonade or orangeade.

JUNE

A TREE PICNIC

Naturally, this will be an outdoor affair in a place where there are lots of trees. Beware of poison ivy and oak.

Tree Identification: Pair off and provide each couple with a pencil and a card with a list of numbers corresponding to numbers on various trees. Each couple is to write the name of each tagged tree opposite its number on the card. When all have finished they return and the leader reads the correct list, each couple checking its own answers.

Tree Leaves: Couples change partners and scout the woods to find leaves. The couple who gathers the largest collection of different varieties of tree leaves are declared Leaf Champions. They must be able to name the tree to which a leaf belongs before being allowed to count it.

Leaf Identification: The crowd now sits on the ground in a circle, and the leader passes around a collection of leaves from various trees. Those leaves have numbers pinned on them. The couples write the names of the trees opposite their numbers. The leader reads the correct list.

Tree Bark: The same thing is done with bits of tree bark. It will add interest if a good woodcraftsman is present to explain how to identify trees.

Do You Know Your Wood? The same plan can be followed with polished pieces of wood—cherry, oak, maple, pine, gum, beech, hickory, walnut. It may be possible to get tiny samples from the lumber yard.

Spatter Prints: Have someone demonstrate spatter printing and have enough equipment on hand to give everyone a chance to print a few leaves on white sheets of paper. You will need some showcard tempera or ink (green, red, blue), a number of old toothbrushes, an equal number of pieces of wire screen three by five inches, and a few pins to hold the leaves and paper in place.

Tree Anagrams: Stand the group in line. The leader calls out a letter—for instance, *B*. The first person in line must call the name of a tree beginning with that letter. Perhaps the player says "Beech." Then the next player says "Balsam," or "Banana," or "Butternut." When a player cannot answer with the name of a tree that has not been mentioned and some other player below in the line can, the player must go to the end while the successful player takes his or her place. Each player must get a chance in turn. When no one can answer, the leader calls another letter, and the game proceeds.

What Good Is Wood? Have the players sit in a circle. Each player, in turn, must mention some use we make of trees. When a use has been named, it cannot be called again. If desired, players may be required to drop out when they fail to respond. Suggestions: for shade; to produce apples, peaches, pears, prunes, cherries, nuts; to build houses, sheds, stables, barns, chairs, tables, beds, etc; to make fires, to make pencils, to absorb water, to prevent floods.

Bible References: It would be interesting if someone is prepared to call attention to the number of references to trees in the Bible. Any good concordance will give this information. See Deut. 20:19; Job 14:7; Psalm 1:3; Eccles. 11:3; Ezek. 31:1-9.

A Vesper Service: Have the group gather in a large circle. Hand a piece of string 101½ feet long to the leader and have it passed along until everyone is holding the string. Expand the circle until it is 101½ feet in circumference. Relate the following fact about this circle: This is the size of the largest tree in the world. Ask if anyone can name the tree. (The answer is the General Sherman Tree.) Ask where the tree is located. (It is located in California.) What kind of tree is the General Sherman? (It is a Redwood.)

The group then forms a circle around a tree that has been sawed down. If such a tree is unavailable, a drawing of a tree showing the rings will suffice. Relate to the group that the rings tell a story. By counting the rings, one can tell the age of the tree. The distance between the rings shows whether there were rainy seasons or dry seasons. If the tree was injured or ill during a year, scars will appear to show this. When a tree stops growing, it dies.

When we as Christians stop growing, we also die. We wear the scars of illness and injury due to sin in our lives. We cannot hide the bad years, just as the tree cannot hide the bad years. If we do not continue to grow spiritually through Bible study, worship, prayer, assembling together, we stop growing. Like the tree that needs nourishment, we too need the nourishment of being actively involved in our church.

Tree Riddles:
Which is the straightest tree? Plum
Which tree is made of stone? Lime
Which tree is older than others? Elder
Which tree languishes? Pine
Which tree is found after a fire? Ash
Which tree keeps a lady warm? Fir
Which tree is often kept in bottles? Cork
Which tree is homely? Plane
Which tree do you carry in your hand? Palm
What tree reminds you of a couple? Pear
What tree suggests your sweetheart? Peach
What tree is sticky, but good to chew? Gum
What tree suggests a color? Redwood
What tree suggests clothes? Cottonwood
What tree is an insect? Locust

Refreshments—Serve Cheesy Walnut Pinwheels* and beverage.

A JUNE JUBILEE PARTY

Rose Garden: Players are seated in a circle. One player, IT, stands in the center. The entire group numbers off by fours. All ones are Red Roses; all twos, White Roses; all threes, American Beauties; and all fours, Ramblers. IT says, "I want a bouquet of Red Roses and Ramblers." All Red Roses and Ramblers change seats, while IT endeavors to get a seat. The player who is left standing is IT and the game proceeds, the player calling the names of any two kinds of roses. When IT calls out "Garden Gate," all players must change seats.

Rose Relay: The Red and White Roses combine against the Ramblers and American Beauties for all contests. Two teams of ten players each are chosen for the relay. These two teams line up facing each other, their players placed so that the lines stretch the length of the room. A rose is given to the player at the head of each line. At the signal to start, this player must zigzag in and out of the line and back, then pass the rose to the next player in line. That player immediately starts down the line in the same fashion, going to the foot of the line, the head, and back to position before passing the rose to the next teammate. The first team to have all its runners complete the course wins.

Knot Contest: Five to ten players for each team. Two strings the length of the room, each containing as many tight knots as there are members on each team. Player Number One runs to the first knot, unties it, and runs back to touch off the next teammate. Number Two takes the next knot, and so on, the idea being to see which team can be first to untie every knot on its string.

Matrimonial Difficulties: Two or three couples from each side. Tie ends of long pieces of string to the wrists of each girl. The boys then have a string tied to one wrist, looped under his partner's string, and tied to the other wrist. The idea is to see which side's players can get out of this double-handcuff first, without breaking the string.

Refreshments—Serve Hurry Pie* and beverage.

JULY

A BALLOON PARTY

Balloon-making Contest: Quite a bit of interest can be aroused in a balloon-making contest, all the balloons to be made of tissue paper. Ingenuity, beauty, and efficiency will be taken into consideration by the judges in rendering their decision. Efficiency is rated by the ability of the balloon to function properly. This would be tested by actually sending the balloons up. Quite a feature could be made of this part of the program.

Fan Ball: Divide the group into two sides. Have teams of from five to ten players each to represent the sides. Each player is provided with a fan and players take positions similar to those in basketball. The field is fifty by twenty-five feet. The referee starts the game by blowing a whistle and tossing the balloon in the air between the two centers, who try to knock it to one of their teammates. The idea of the game is to get the ball over the opponent's goal line. After each score the ball is brought back to center and tossed up as before. Ten points is considered a game.

When the ball goes outside or touches the floor the referee blows a whistle and tosses it up between two opposing players at the point where it went out or touched the floor. If a balloon should burst, the referee should provide another, tossing it up at that point. All strokes must be made with the fan. No player may run with the balloon or hit it with the free hand. It must be batted through the air. Ping-pong paddles may be substituted for fans.

Balloon Burst: Have a number of large balloons. The long ones will be good for this purpose. Paint ridiculous faces on the ends. Have several representatives from each group contest. Each begins blowing up a balloon on the signal to start. The winner is the one whose balloon bursts first. Each player should continue to blow until the balloon bursts.

(For other balloon games, see *The New Fun Encyclopedia,* Vol. I, *Games.*)

Refreshments—Banana-split Cake* and beverage.

JULY FOURTH PICNIC

Publicity—Flags everywhere help emphasize the theme of this party. Large banners painted in red and blue on strips of butcher paper or newsprint can announce this old-fashioned picnic.

Program

Three-Legged Race: After the teams have been selected, choose a male and a female to represent each team. Tie the right leg of one to the left leg of the other with a strong cloth around the knees. Have them race from the starting line to the finish line.

Wheelbarrow Race: Select two males to represent each team. Player One grabs Player Two by the ankles as Player Two rests on the palms of the hands. In wheelbarrow fashion, they race from the starting line to the finish line.

Sack Race: Select a representative from each team. Each player places both feet in a large burlap potato sack and holds the sack up with the hands. On the signal, the players hop from the starting line to the finish line.

Casting for Accuracy: Have enough fishing rods with reels for each contestant. An old tire, a balloon, or some other target is placed a good distance from the casting line. Each player gets five chances to cast the *hookless* lure into the tire, or hit the balloon or other target. A point is scored each time the target is hit.

Softball Toss: Each team provides a player to toss a softball for distance.

Frisbee Toss: Players toss frisbees for accuracy.

Tug-O-War: Provide a large rope and let the teams pull against each other until one team is pulled across the goal line. For fun, dig a large hole and fill with water. The winning team is the one *not* pulled into the muddy waterhole.

Refreshments—There is nothing better than fried chicken, potato salad, baked beans, ice-cold lemonade (made the old-fashioned way with lemons), and either homemade ice cream or ice-cold watermelon.

PATRIOTIC PARTY

Decorations—Plan this event for the birthday of a president or the Fourth of July. Decorate with red, white, and blue crepe-paper streamers, American flags, and political posters.

Program

Mixer: As guests arrive, hand each a slip of paper with a song title written on it. This will determine the group each guest will join. If there are to be four groups, then there should be just four song titles: "America, the Beautiful," "Dixie," "My Country, 'Tis of Thee," "The Star-Spangled Banner," or "Yankee Doodle." When all guests have arrived, instruct them to hum or sing their songs and find others singing the same song to form teams. Each team should choose a name. Limit these names to historical figures or political parties. Suggestions: Lincoln's Lovers, Washington's War Eagles, Franklin's Fantastics, Democratic Demons.

American History: Each team sits together. The leader holds up an A card. The first person to shout out a famous

historical event or person whose name begins with the
letter A wins that card for his or her team. The leader holds
up a card for each letter of the alphabet. The group that
collects the most cards wins.

Nickname Identification: The leader asks the nickname
of states. If Alabama is called out, the first person to give
the correct nickname for Alabama wins a point for his or
her team. Allow a few seconds for answers. If no one
answers, give the correct answer and call the next state.
The team with the most correct answers wins. Here is a list
of states and nicknames:

Alabama (Cotton State)
Alaska (Seward's Ice Box, America's Ice Box, or The
    Frozen Wilderness)
Arizona (Grand Canyon State)
Arkansas (The Land of Opportunity)
California (Golden State)
Colorado (Centennial State)
Connecticut (Constitution State)
Delaware (Diamond State)
Florida (Sunshine State)
Georgia (Empire State of the South or Peach State)
Hawaii (Aloha State)
Idaho (Gem State)
Illinois (Land of Lincoln)
Indiana (Hoosier State)
Iowa (Hawkeye State)
Kansas (Sunflower State)
Kentucky (Bluegrass State)
Louisiana (Pelican State)
Maine (Pine Tree State)
Maryland (Old Line State)
Massachusetts (Bay State)
Michigan (Wolverine State)
Minnesota (Gopher State)
Mississippi (Magnolia State)

Missouri (Show Me State)
Montana (Treasure State)
Nebraska (Corn Husker State or Tree Planter State)
Nevada (Silver State)
New Hampshire (Granite State)
New Jersey (Garden State)
New Mexico (The Land of Enchantment)
New York (Empire State)
North Carolina (Tarheel State)
North Dakota (Flickertail State)
Ohio (Buckeye State)
Oklahoma (Sooner State)
Oregon (Beaver State)
Pennsylvania (Keystone State)
Rhode Island (Little Rhody)
South Carolina (Palmetto State)
South Dakota (Sunshine State)
Tennessee (Volunteer State)
Texas (Lone Star State)
Utah (Beehive State)
Vermont (Green Mountain State)
Virginia (The Mother of Presidents)
Washington (Evergreen State)
West Virginia (Mountain State)
Wisconsin (Badger State)
Wyoming (Equality State)

Who Said It? Another question and answer game, but one in which the whole group can participate. Give each person a copy of the questions below and a pencil. Guests may help one another with this quiz. Each quote is by a famous historical person. Choose from the names below, placing the correct letter beside the quotation.

____ 1. "Do not conceive that fine clothes make fine men, anymore than fine feathers make fine birds."

____ 2. "I think this is the most extraordinary collection of talent, of human knowledge, that has ever been

gathered at the White House—with the possible
exception of when Thomas Jefferson dined alone."

____ 3. "Speak softly and carry a big stick."

____ 4. "The only thing we have to fear is fear itself."

____ 5. "Eat to please thyself, but dress to please others."

____ 6. "The White House is the finest prison in the
world."

____ 7. "With malice toward none, with charity for all,
with firmness in the right as God gives us to see the
right, let us finish the work we are in."

____ 8. "I never met a man I didn't like."

____ 9. "I thank God for my handicaps, for through them, I
have found myself, my work, and my God."

____10. "I was born an American; I live an American. I
shall die an American."

A. Helen Keller   B. Franklin Roosevelt
C. Daniel Webster   D. Harry Truman
E. George Washington   F. Abraham Lincoln
G. Theodore Roosevelt   H. John F. Kennedy
I. Benjamin Franklin   J. Will Rogers

Answers:

(1) E–George Washington   (2) H–John F. Kennedy
(3) G–Theodore Roosevelt   (4) B–Franklin Roosevelt
(5) I–Benjamin Franklin   (6) D–Harry Truman
(7) F–Abraham Lincoln   (8) J–Will Rogers
(9) A–Helen Keller   (10) C–Daniel Webster

Devotional—Conclude with a devotional on the freedom
of religion, which is guaranteed by our Constitution.

Refreshments—Serve homemade ice cream. Have bananas, nuts, and syrups available to further enhance this
treat.

Adapted from Bob and Carolyn Sessoms, *52 Complete Recreation
Programs for Senior Adults* (Nashville: Convention Press, 1979),
pp. 55-56. Used by permission.

AUGUST

A HIRAM AND MIRANDY PARTY

Three different plans are suggested for developing this party. Take your choice or use a combination of the three.

Invitations

Hiram, Hiram, I've been thinking
Just what great fun it would be
If you'd bring Miss ———
Friday evening to see me.

Overalls, a red bandana,
Instead of a necktie a big straw hat,
Leave your city ways behind you,
Come prepared for a reg'lar bat.

———

Mirandy, Mirandy, I've been thinking
Just what great fun it would be
If you'd come next Friday evening
With Mr. ——— to see me.

Wear your apron and sunbonnet,
Lunch is needed, that's a fact;
Leave your city ways behind you,
Come prepared for a reg'lar bat.

Plan I (Outdoors)—The group gathers at the place designated by the leader. Announcement is made that transportation will be provided for all. No one knows the destination of the group but the leader. When they are all assembled they are informed that each person's feet are to be the transportation provided. The group then follows the leader.

Mystery Ramble: When they have gone some distance they stop, line up single file, and are told to proceed with as little noise as possible. Thus they follow until the leader brings them to a spot where a campfire is burning. Seats have been arranged council fashion.

Discoveries: After they are seated one of the leaders explains that they are in a strange land and weaves a fanciful story of romances, Indians, pirates, treasures, the world of outer space, etc. Each person is then given fifteen minutes to go out and bring in some memento significant of those adventurous days. Ingenious and imaginative hunters may find some remarkable exhibits. One may come back with a knob off the ark, another with a leaf from the Garden of Eden, another with a feather from the bonnet of Pocahontas, another with the stone David used to slay Goliath, another with a jewel from Captain Kidd's treasure.

At the end of the allotted time the leader blows a whistle and all return. Each person is required to display a trophy and tell its story, explaining what it is, how it came to be in this place, how the person obtained it, and something of its history.

Plan II (Indoors or Outdoors)—*Howdy Hiram! Howdy, Mirandy!* This is the stock greeting for the evening, and the only one used as people meet.

Pin the Tail on the Donkey: This old one needs no explanation.

Farmer Brown: One player starts by saying something like this:

> Farmer Brown went to town
> Riding on a pony;
> Came back home, all alone,
> With a lot of Bologna.

This is correct, for the player's name is Baker. It begins with a *B* and so does Bologna.

It should be explained that each player is expected to answer in rhyme, when at all possible. If unable to answer in rhyme, the player is to tell what Farmer Brown brought from town, at any rate. It will add to the fun if the players are not warned that the articles mentioned must begin with player's last initial. When they answer incorrectly, they are informed that they are wrong. Suggestions for rhyming lines 2 and 4 when the player's last name begins with A or B:

A

> Farmer Brown went to town
> With a Ford he grapples;
> Came back home, all alone,
> With a load of Apples.

B

> Farmer Brown went to town
> Up and down the wide streets;
> Came back home, all alone,
> With a dozen red Beets.

Other suggested rhymes for lines 2 and 4, from C through Z: C (savages, cabbages) D (wishes, dishes) E (legs, eggs) F (hour, flour) G (train, grain) H (tow sack, hardtack) I (nice, ice) J (lakes, johnny cakes) K (lout, kraut) L (weather, leather) M (sunny, money) N (bag, nag) O (bargain, organ) P (sizes, prizes) Q (princes, quinces) R (steeds, reeds) S (spots, scots) T (measure, treasure) U (yellow, umbrella) V (ran, van) W (rig, wig) Y (barn, yarn) Z (hero, zero)

Number Change: Players are seated in a circle and number off in fives. There are enough seats for all the players except one. The player who is IT announces that the numbers represent farms and that the numbers called must change locations. IT will try to get a farm (seat) in the scramble. Because there are several people with the same number, there will be four or more players changing each time. The player left without a farm becomes IT.

Spelling Bee: Divide into two equal sides and conduct an old-fashioned spelling bee.

Here are ten difficult words that are likely to trip even the best of spellers: rarefy, liquefier, supersede, naphtha, sacrilegious, paraffin, kimono, tranquillity, picnicking, battalion.

If there are players on each side still standing, here are fifty more:

appendicitis	capillary	ghoul
asafetida	chrysalis	gnome
acetylene	columbarium	gnomology
baccalaureate	ecclesiastic	geranium
believe	eclectic	hauteur
caoutchouc	fossiliferous	hautboy
hallucination	oleomargarine	stationery
isobar	onyx	stereopticon
innuendo	periphery	sycophant
latitudinarian	pharmaceutical	synagogue
mademoiselle	personnel	synchronous
marvelous	physiognomy	syzygy
maraschino	psychology	tautological
meningitis	puissance	toxic
mignonette	punctilious	turquoise
miscellaneous	receive	valetudinarian
nonchalance	rendezvous	

Refreshments—Assorted fruit dish, with a variety of fruit juices.

A GLOBE-TROTTER'S PARTY

Spend about twenty minutes at each house.

First House—Japan: Hostesses in costume. Each guest removes shoes before going in, and guests sit on the floor.

Decorations: All furniture removed, pillows placed on floor, Japanese lanterns.

Program: Play Gossip, using this sentence: A Japanese warrior sang to his Japanese girl, "OWHA TAGOO SIAM." She replied, "So you are!"

Refreshments: Tea and crackers.

Second House—France: Hostesses in costume.

Decorations: Small tables with checkered cloths, cabaret style.

Program: Short musical program.

Refreshments: Ginger ale or punch.

Third House—Mexico: Hostesses in costume.

Decorations: Few Spanish shawls.

Program: Mexican fortunetellers and Mexican music.

Refreshments: Hot tamales and crackers.

Fourth House—Fantasyland: Two girls dressed as fantasy characters to greet guests.

Decorations: Nursery. All furniture removed. Toys.

Program: Play jacks, blocks, checkers, etc., on floor.

Refreshments: Lollipops and bubble gum.

Church—Dixie: Watermelons served in abundance. Songs.

A GYPSY PARTY

Invitations

> Oh, would you be a roamer,
> And with the roamers roam?
> Then hie yourself to Funland,
> And to our party come.

Guests should be requested to attend in gypsy costume. A bright-colored bandana and sash will answer the purpose. Some of these could be provided.

Mimeographed programs in decorated covers could be given each guest. Some of your young people who are clever with water colors could be pressed into service. Landscapes, campfire scenes, gypsy heads, or magazine pictures may be used to decorate them. The name of the party, organization, place, and date should be indicated. These would serve as excellent mementos.

Program

1. The Gypsy Trail
   "We're not stringing you."

2. The Gypsy Fortuneteller
   "Sees all! Knows all!"

3. Gypsy Frolic
   "Be lively and happy."

4. Gypsy Tents
   "Scoot!"

5. The Gypsy Court
   "It's a secret!"

6. A Gypsy Daisy
   "Daisies sometimes tell."

7. The Gypsy Camp Sing
   "Now, everybody."

8. Gypsy Partners
   "Knife 'em!"

9. Gypsy Treasure
   "Oh, boy!"

The Gypsy Trail: Each guest selects the end of a string from a bunch of strings at the porch and follows it to its end. It crosses and tangles with other strings, zigzagging back and forth until it leads the holder to the goal. On the end of the string there is a fortune which indicates the guest's future fate.

The Gypsy Fortuneteller: Fix up a gypsy fortunetelling tent on the lawn. If you can find someone who knows something of palmistry, much of the success of the evening's program is assured. If not available, provide the "gypsy" with slips of paper on which are written fortunes in invisible ink (lemon juice). These are passed over a lighted candle until the heat brings out the message.

Gypsy Frolic: The players form a circle with two or three players inside. These players walk about as everyone sings the verse of the song below (to tune of "This is the Way We Wash Our Clothes"). As they come to the chorus they stand in front of some player and curtsy. They then grasp that player's hands, skating position, and on the chorus, skip about inside the circle together. All players in the circle remain stationary, but all sing. As the next verse is started, partners drop hands and again walk about inside the ring. This time, on reaching the chorus, each new player on the inside also takes a partner. The game continues until all players have been taken from the circle.

As I was walking down the street,
Heigho-heigho, heigho-heigho!
A gypsy (girl) (boy) I chanced to meet,
Heigho-heigho! Heigho-heigho!

CHORUS:
Rig-ajig-jig, and away we go,
Away we go, away we go!
Rig-ajig-jig, and away we go,
Hiegho! Heigho! Heigho!

Gypsy Tents: Players form groups of three. Two of these players hold hands, while the third gets inside, as in London Bridge Is Falling Down. The two players form the tent, the third is a gypsy. There ought to be several extra gypsies. At the signal, every gypsy gets out of one tent and scoots for another. The extra gypsies endeavor to get a tent in the scramble. Play rapidly for about five minutes.

The Gypsy Court: A throne has been arranged by draping two chairs. The committee has selected a King and Queen of the Gypsies. The court is called to order by the leader who explains the game. In the possession of the Queen is a red bandana handkerchief. Some boy is required to go to the throne, bow to the Queen, and receive from her that handkerchief. He must then do with it what she whispers to him to do! He must keep this order a secret, simply obeying her wishes. For instance, the Queen may tell him to give the handkerchief to the prettiest girl at the party. He makes his selection and proceeds to tie the bandana handkerchief loosely about the girl's neck. The girl then must go to the throne and bow before the King. He may whisper into her ear that she must give the handkerchief to the boy who would make the best husband. When she has decided, she ties the bandana about the boy's neck and he appears before the Queen. So it goes until most of the players have been given this privilege. Then the leader announces that all players must tell to whom they gave the handkerchiefs and why they gave it. There may be some blushing and much laughter, but each player is required to tell the secret. The handkerchief may be given for the prettiest eyes, the best conversationalist, the smartest, the sweetest, the biggest ears, the loudest, the hungriest, the most lovable, etc. The girls always go to the King and the boys to the Queen.

A Gypsy Daisy: The Gypsy Queen has been provided with a beautiful wand. The wand is made of a light stick about two and one-half feet long, on the end of which has been tacked or taped two cardboard discs about four inches in diameter. The rod is covered with green crepe paper, and the discs with orange or deep yellow. Each disc is covered separately for there must be space between them for the insertion of the daisy petals. Each petal is doubled. Inside it is written a fortune or fate. The petals are inserted between the two discs and held in place by a pin. One at a time, the players appear before the Queen. She extends her wand, and each player pulls one of the petals and reads it to the entire group. If the crowd is too large for everyone to have a chance in The Gypsy Court, then the players left out are to be given first chance at the Gypsy Daisy.

The Gypsy Camp Sing: If a real campfire is not possible, then one should be improvised by using a flashlight, some red crepe paper (or theatrical gelatin), and some sticks.

Have someone with a guitar dress as a gypsy and play as the group sings around the campfire.

Gypsy Partners: After a short sing announce that all the men are going to knife their partners. Write the name of each girl on a slip of paper. Place these slips on the ground, face down. The men step forward, are given a long-bladed, sharp-pointed knife, and told to stick a name by dropping the knife from waist height. Each man thus "knifes" his partner. Should this party be held indoors, a soft-wood board or some other material should be provided for the "knifings."

Gypsy Treasure: Each man and his partner are now given a map to find a "gypsy treasure." They follow directions on this map and finally come to the place where the treasure is hidden, probably under a rock, in a porch corner, or under a piano cover. The treasure proves to be a tiny match box containing a slip of paper. It tells the couple to present this slip to the refreshment committee for a reward. No couple should be served until it finds its treasure or makes an earnest effort to do so. Several special treasures should be hidden to add interest to the search. Dime-store necklaces would make splendid treasures. Those who hide the treasures should draw charts of the locations.

Refreshments—Chicken wing appetizers, Biscuits*, Chocolate-chip Oatmeal Cookies*, and beverage.

SEPTEMBER

A FUN-SCHOOL PARTY

Invitations

Come to our party, a Big Fun School,
Don't bring your books, it's against the rule.

Program

Sculpture: On arrival each person is furnished with a piece of Ivory soap. If desired, you may ask guests to bring their own soap. A knife is also necessary. Models are placed about the room, and each person carves some bit of statuary. As the pieces are finished they are placed on display. An award may be given for the best. Be sure to have plenty of newspapers on hand so the carvers can keep their shavings off of the floor.

Arithmetic

1. Numberology. To the ancients, numbers had great significance. Even in our day superstitions about numbers persist. Thirteen is unlucky. Some hotels have no thirteenth floor, because so many guests refuse to be placed on that floor. In baseball there is the "lucky seventh" inning when every rooter stands and expects something to happen. Lower seven was considered the lucky berth on a train's sleeping car.

Numerology is an old form of fortunetelling by numbers. Guests are given an opportunity to work out their own fortunes. In a small crowd, someone may do it for them, announcing the result to the group. Each letter has a significance:

1	2	3	4	5	6	7	8	9
A	B	C	D	E	F	G	H	I
J	K	L	M	N	O	P	Q	R
S	T	U	V	W	X	Y	Z	

Example:	6	9	15	1 plus 5	6
	John Smith		—	———	—
	1 85 1 4 28		29	2 plus 9	11

Each letter has a numerical value. The values of the vowels are placed above the name, the consonants below. They are added, and then the digits of the result are added. The final result indicates the fortune. If it should amount to more than thirteen, then add the two digits again. Thus the name is reduced to the key numbers. These indicate the character reading of the person.

The key: (1) creative ability (2) action (3) executive ability (4) love of detail (5) strength of character (6) thinker, meditative (7) aggressive (8) care of others, unselfish, domestic (9) emotional power, dramatic ability (10) kind, considerate of others (11) artistic sense (12) imagination (13) troublemaker

Thus 6 shows John Smith to be a thinker and meditative, and 11 shows he is a man of artistic sense.

2. Living Numbers: The crowd is divided into two or more sides for the various events that are to follow. Players are furnished with numbers from 0 to 9, one number to each player. The sides face one another. The leader calls out certain problems in arithmetic, such as, "How much is 2 plus 2?" The first side to have 4 step forward is awarded a point. "How many cakes in a baker's dozen?" This time 1 and 3 must stand together in front of the line. More difficult problems may be given. Or the leader may throw in questions regarding historic events, such as "When did Columbus discover America?"

Reading: One or two persons are elected from each group. The leader has written the names of certain nursery rhymes on slips of paper. The readers draw one slip each. They are then required to recite that particular rhyme, omitting every fourth word. The rhyme must be recited without undue hesitation, and if a reader puts in a fourth word, points are awarded the opponents. Thus "Mary Had a Little Lamb" would be recited in this fashion:

> Mary had a ——— lamb,
> Its fleece ——— white as snow,
> ——— everywhere that Mary ———,
> The lamb was ——— to go.

The reader might be required to whistle at each fourth word.

Dramatics: The groups present the names of states in charades, taking turns. Easy ones are Pennsylvania (pencil-vain-you), Tennessee (ten-s-see), Arkansas (ark-and-saw or r-can-saw), Illinois (ill-annoy), Maryland (merry-land), Colorado (color-add-oh).

History

1. Each group is given some historic event to illustrate by a drawing on the chalkboard. The other groups try to guess what event is represented by the drawing.

2. The leader has slips of paper with various events written on them. The groups draw one slip each, then illustrate the events in turn. The crowd tries to guess the event portrayed. Suggestions: Washington crossing the Delaware; Lindberg crossing the Atlantic; Paul Revere's ride; George Washington and the cherry tree.

Geography: Fifteen beanbags are needed. On each beanbag is pinned the name of a city. On a large paper or cardboard, states are blocked off in eight-inch squares. The idea is to get each city in its own state by tossing the beanbag from a distance of about ten feet. A miss means that the player has to throw again until the city lands in the proper state. The group having the lowest number of tries wins. If a beanbag lands on a line between two states, it is counted as being in the state which holds the most of it.

English: Give everyone pencil and paper. See who can make the most words from the letters in the word *education.*

Spelling: Play the familiar Living Alphabet, or play Discovered Words. Words are written out and then cut into single letters. All letters in a given word have the same number. Thus in the word *Quarrel,* each letter is numbered 1. That makes it possible for all the players who are numbered one to get together for this word. Next they

discover what the word is. They then present the word to
the crowd in dramatic form. The rest of the players try to
guess the word. Suggested words: football, baseball,
automobile, chorus, opera, quartet, movies, propose,
airplane, school.

Refreshments—Eskimo pies or ice-cream cones.

A GIVE-AWAY PARTY

Invitations—Request that everyone bring some dis-
carded garment or garments—things they are willing to
give away—hats, shoes, dresses, suits, caps, sweaters, etc.
These should be wrapped. At the close of the party they are
to be distributed to the needy.

Give Away: When the party starts each person is told to
carry his or her bundle in the grand march that is to follow.
The girls form a line on one side of the room, the boys on the
other. As the music plays they march down the sides of the
room and across to the middle, coming down the middle by
couples. They march around by twos into a circle. At the
signal, the inner circle reverses and marches in the
opposite direction, the outer circle continuing as before. At
the second signal the two circles stop and face each other.
Each person in the inner circle pairs off with one in the
outer circle, and the partners exchange packages.

Players immediately open their packages and must put
on the garments and wear them for the rest of the evening.
It's just too bad if Mary Jones gets a pair of large oxfords
that used to grace the big feet of Bob Brown. Imagine the
hilarity of the group when husky Ed Clark opens his
package and dons a cute little baby cap.

Follow this by playing give-away games.

Penny: Pass article or articles to the right, giving them
away as fast as possible. At the signal, players holding the
"pennies" drop out of the circle.

Secret Handshakers: One or more people in the crowd are secretly given pennies. They are instructed that the fifth person who shakes hands with them must be given the pennies. They may continue until the leader blows a whistle. At that time the players holding the pennies may keep them.

Give-away Beans: Each player is given ten beans. Whenever a player can get another player to answer any question with yes or no, that player must be given a bean. The idea is to get rid of all ten beans by giving them away to others.

Percolate: One player goes out of the room. The others select some verb such as *sneeze* or *snore* or *smile* or *sing* or *cook.* The player sent out of the room comes back and tries to discover the word by asking questions to which the players are required to answer truthfully yes or no. In framing these questions the word *percolate* must be used for the verb selected by the group. "Do you percolate?" "Do you percolate at night?" "Do you percolate frequently?" "Do you like to percolate?"

The player who "gives away" the word by his answer is selected to go out next.

Who's the Leader? (Look for the "give-away.") One person leads the group in what it is doing, while another player in the center of the circle tries to discover who the leader is. Players clap their hands, jump, wave, or do whatever the leader does. It will add to the fun if the game is played to music.

Pinchee—No Laughee: (Don't give it away.) Players are seated in a circle. The leader turns to the player on the right, pinches both cheeks of that person, and says solemnly, "Pinchee—no laughee." That person turns to the player on the right and repeats the action. On the next round, the players put the forefinger of one hand under the chin of the person to the right and say "Chuck-a-luckee."

On the third round they run the fingers down the face of the person and say "Cootchie-cootchie."

The trick is soon apparent to all but one of the players. One player's fingers are covered with soot or black chalk and leave marks on the face of the player to the right.

Give-away Packages: Several players are given packages which they are told must be given away to other players. A player does not have to take the package and can only be made to do so by being tricked into answering yes or no to some question. After the game has been played a brief time, the leader should have received one of the packages. The leader then proceeds to open the package and start eating, for it contains a piece of candy, or a sandwich, or something of the sort. Then players who passed up a package will be sorry.

Refreshments—Chicken-salad sandwiches and fruit punch.

WORLD SERIES FELLOWSHIP

Publicity—Announce that this event is to take place just before the World Series. Invite guests to appear in your organization's World Series.

This fellowship should take place in a fellowship hall or large room. Divide the group into two equal teams, naming them for the American League and National League teams appearing in the particular year's World Series.

Each team will participate in the following activities to see who will win the World Series:

First Inning

Ping-pong Carry: Each player receives a plastic soup spoon. The teams line up single file. The first player in each team holds the spoon between the teeth and places a ping-pong ball in the spoon. Without touching the spoon with the hands, the player gently walks the course, carrying the ping-pong ball in the spoon. If the ball drops out, the player picks it up, places it back in the spoon, and continues to walk the course.

The course consists of a string hung across the course at a height of four feet, for the player to walk under, and another string hung across the course at a height of two feet, for the player to step over. On the signal, the first player on each team walks the course under and over the strings, goes to a chair, sits down, gets back up, walks the course back to the starting point, and, using no hands, gently passes the ping-pong ball to the second player by tilting his or her own spoon so the ball rolls into the other player's spoon. If the ball falls, the player is to replace it in the spoon and make another attempt to pass it. When the ball is in the second player's spoon, that player walks the course. This continues until all have completed the course. The winning team gets a point for this inning.

Second Inning

Run the Bases: Each team is lined up in single file. The first players on each team are given large balloons to carry between their knees. On the signal, they are to hop or walk from the starting point, around an object, and return. The rest of the players repeat the action. The first team to complete the course wins a point for this inning.

Third Inning—Each team lines up single file, all players an arm's length apart. All players stand with their feet wide apart. The leader of each team has a volleyball (or basketball) which is passed or rolled between the legs of all the players, in an attempt to get the ball to the last player. When the last player receives the ball, all players should step back one step. The last player then rushes to the front of the line and rolls the ball through the legs to the last person, who repeats the action. When the first player returns to the front of the line, the game is over. One point for the winning team.

Add the scores to see which team wins your World Series.

Refreshments—What else? Hot dogs, chips, pretzels, and soft drinks.

OCTOBER

HALLOWEEN SOCIAL

Invitations—These may be written or typed in black on orange paper, which is then cut into pumpkin shapes. On the front a black cut-out of a witch can be pasted and the invitation written on the reverse side.

Another kind may be made by mounting the outline of a bony white hand on black paper, postcard size, and typing or writing the invitation across the hand.

> The spectral hand of Halloween,
> With eerie and uncanny mien
> Bids you welcome to its fete
> Where ghosts and witches you will greet
> And much, I'm sure, to your surprise,
> They'll penetrate through your disguise
> And guide you through the secret pass
> That leads you to their haunt, alas!
> Enough is said—do not delay
> By eight at ———
> They'll hold full sway.
> Date———

Decorations—Guests should meet at a spot a short distance from the party. This could be at the church, on someone's front porch, or in a side or backyard. The meeting place should present a dark spooky appearance.

Jack-o'-lanterns or battery-operated lamps should be used, with moss, bare branches, and shocks of corn. Moss can be hung from lines that extend from one end of the room or yard to the other.

The home or assembly room in which the party is to be held should be appropriately decorated in orange and black with long sheets of orange crepe-paper forming curtains upon which have been pasted black cut-outs— bats, cats, owls, and witches. To divide rooms, apples may be attached to rows of strings. These can be used for bobbing later. Corn shocks, branches, etc., fill the corners and may be supplemented here and there with witches, spooks, and scarecrows. Cover the lights with orange crepe paper upon which have been pasted bats, etc.

Weird jack-o'-lanterns and masks should hang everywhere. In a corner of the room a witch's cave can be made by turning a kitchen table on its side with the top to the wall and covering the legs with gray crepe paper to form the sides, draping it with vines and leaves.

Program—At the meeting place, several ghosts and witches should hand guests small Halloween cut-outs, numbered 1, 2, 3, or 4. There should be about the same number of people in each group. The guests assemble in their various groups and await instructions. Each group is given a slip of paper, apparently blank, but by holding the slip over a lighted candle, which the ghosts will furnish, they will find instructions: "Make a wild dash for the drugstore," "Stop when you reach second and third streets," "Beware lest you tarry at the Big Oak." These instructions have been previously written in lemon juice on each slip of paper.

As soon as their directions are read the groups start out to their given spots. There they receive further instructions from another ghost or witch. The groups make as many stops as deemed necessary to reach the goal, which is the Halloween party itself, each group taking a different course. The first group to reach the party is presented with a small sack of candy corn.

Upon arrival, guests are presented to the "master ghost," who shakes hands. To their horror, the hand comes off as they clasp it. This can be done by stuffing a white rubber glove with wet corn meal. Leave the wrist unstuffed so that the ghost's hand may be inserted. Tie a long string around the ghost's arm and to the edge of the glove. This will leave the hand dangling when released.

Dance of the Witches: Form two concentric circles, boys on the outside, girls on the inside. If more girls than boys, extra girls pair off, half on outer and half on inner circle. One player marches in center of circle with a broom. A lively march is played as couples march around. When whistle blows, the inner circle reverses and both circles continue to march until the player in the center drops the broom and makes a dash for a partner. The player left out is IT next time.

Pumpkin Plunking: A row of ten different-sized pumpkins are cut out of cardboard, decorated, and strung up. The largest pumpkin is at one end of the row and smallest at the other. Explain that each pumpkin counts the number of points marked on it. The largest 5, then 10, 15, and so on to the smallest, 50. Use the four groups already assembled, or group the guests in two teams, according to your crowd. A line is marked off twenty feet away from the pumpkins. The two sides stand in parallel lines behind the mark. Give a small ball to the first in line, who tosses it at the pumpkins and returns the ball to the first person in the second line, and so on, the groups alternating. The side having the largest score is awarded a bundle of crepe-paper caps, one for each member. If four groups are used, play two at a time, running off a final for the two winning teams.

Ghost Treasure: Draw one small circle in center of floor, and four large circles, equally distant from the center. Let each of the four original groups occupy one of the large circles. This is their home base. A pile of candy or peanuts is placed in the center circle. Cut sufficient 1s, 2s, 3s, and 4s from a calendar to pin on the back of each member of the corresponding groups. Upon the signal, all players run out to take the treasure, carrying away one piece at a time. If a player's number is taken off by an opponent while outside home base, the player is "dead," and out of the game. If more than one peanut is taken, the guilty group is disqualified. Count each group's treasure to determine the winner. All the spoils go to the winning group.

Apple Race: Four contestants from each group. Draw two lines ten feet apart. Half the players from each group line up on opposite sides, making four parallel lines, with teammates facing each other. Give each contestant a toothpick and place an apple in front of the first player of each team. The toothpick must be held in the mouth and the apple pushed to the teammate on the opposite side, who returns it to the other side, player two having stepped up to the front of the line. Player two returns it to opposite side, and so on. If the toothpick breaks, the runner must start over. The victors receive a box of "goblin teeth" (marshmallows).

Bobbing for Apples: It wouldn't be Halloween without large tubs of water for apple bobbing. This should preferably be done out-of-doors. Apples may also be strung on clotheslines. The players' hands should be tied behind their backs.

Fortune Booths: A real-looking gypsy fortuneteller (unknown to the crowd) can prove a big hit by putting common sense and a few hints together to make some startlingly real fortunes. She instructs her visitors to touch one of the articles on the table before her to learn their fate: A pile of gold dust denotes wealth; a needle—spinsterhood or bachelorhood; rice—a wedding; fan—romance; dime—an inheritance; torn rag—poverty; scissors—a short life.

Fortune Wheel: Divide a cardboard wheel into six sections and paint each a different color. Provide a cardboard indicator and hang the wheel on the wall. Make up suitable rhymes for each color and post on the wall nearby. When guests spin the indicator, the color on which the indicator stops tells their fortune.

Bluebeard's Den: Decorate a back room or garage as spookily as possible and drape it to resemble Bluebeard's Den. Toward the back of the room, hang a sheet or curtain, behind which seven girls stand with their heads thrust through holes in the sheet as though hanging on wall. Streaks of red extend from the heads to resemble blood. When a victim (guest) is led in, the heads should shake and groan at intervals. Two ghosts walk silently about the room, tickling the victims with feathers or dropping ice snow on them. The grim tale of the fate of Bluebeard's wives is recited as the victim is shown about the dimly-lighted room—first, the clothes, food (untouched), shoes, jewels, beads hanging on the wall, and finally the storyteller, an Oriental, offers to show them the fatal key and allows them to hold it in their hands, telling them to take special precaution not to drop it or harm will come to them. But the key is connected to an electric battery which gives victims such a shock that they drop the key. The victim is then hurried out lest Bluebeard return, and the next person is called.

Refreshments—Nut cookies, candied apples, and witch's brew (fruit punch).

HARD LUCK HOBO PARTY

Invitations

> Yoo-Hoo! Hoo-Doo! Hobos!
> Want to change your luck?
> Come to Hoo-Doo Hall
> Next Friday the thirteenth at 8:13
> On time is good luck;
> Late is bad luck!

Decorations—Use bad luck emblems for decorations. Guests walk under ladder when entering. Artificial campfire in center of room. Guests sit on logs and boxes.

Program

Lucky Scramble: At 8:13 leader blows whistle and scatters candy kisses on floor. Late comers miss the scramble. Their bad luck!

Lucky Scrawl: Contestants are given pencil and paper and instructed to obtain autographs and phone numbers. The first to get thirteen wins.

Hobo's Potluck: Hobos are given five beans and engage in conversation. When one receives yes or no for answer, that hobo is paid one bean. The first to get thirteen beans is winner.

Lucky Handshake: Three people are given small lucky charms. Hobos are instructed to shake hands with one another, not knowing who has the charms. Those holding the charms are to give them to the thirteenth persons with whom they shake hands.

Hobos Pack Their Kit: Circle formation. Leader begins by saying, "When I pack my kit, I take my comb." Second person repeats the first object and adds another. This continues around the circle. Everyone who forgets an object drops out.

Hobos Go to Court: The cast for this mock court is secretly appointed before the party. Needed are a judge, clerk of court, prosecuting attorney, attorney for the defense, defendant, and at least two witnesses for each side. Encourage the two sides to work up their presentations carefully. The defendant has been accused of working. One witness may testify that the defendant has been seen working. He was leaning out the window, holding a lighted candle so his mother could see to chop the wood. A jury selected from the group weighs all the evidence and brings in a decision.

Hobos View the Remains: This game should not be used with young children. And it would be well to guard against anyone being unduly frightened. Dim the lights so that no one can see clearly. Have a helper stand at each end of a row of guests. The leader, using a flashlight, reads this story of a man named Brown. As the story is read, parts of the "body" are passed by the helpers. The players pass the articles from one to the other until they reach the helper at the other end of the row. The reader pauses long enough for each article to pass the full length of the row before reading the next item.

Once upon a time in this very town
Lived a miserly man whose name was Brown.

Alack and alas, on a Halloween night,
He was terribly murdered because of spite.

And ever since then he has roamed the earth
To warn and to haunt the place of his birth.

Tonight we have some of his restless remains,
So we'll make you acquainted at once with his brains.
(wet natural sponge)

And now your shuddering touch will know
The victim's hair has continued to grow.
(corn silk or yarn)

He heard too well the tinkle of gold,
It's a powerful ear that now you hold.

> (dried apple or peach)

His hand is clammy, cold, and still,
No longer can it shoot to kill.

> (rubber glove filled with wet sand)

His eyes were small, but very keen,
Though the kind deeds of earth they've never seen.

> (peeled grape)

He talked a lot when he was young;
Now you're feeling of his tongue.

> (raw oyster)

He was sly and cruel from the start,
So now you'll feel his bleeding heart.

> (piece of raw liver)

The tendons which helped his strong right arm
We pass to you. Keep them from harm.

> (cooked spaghetti)

The food he ate was coarse and dry,
So his teeth were strong. They'll never die.

> (kernels of corn)

But wait! He comes and stands within.
He's hunting for some friend or kin!
Listen closely, and above his moans
You'll hear the rattle of his bones.

A ghost moves slowly through the darkness, rattling a bunch of clothespins tied loosely together. Exits with a moan. Lights on!

March to Victory: Hobos march before judges. Best costumed boy and girl receive red bandanas as prizes.

Strolling Fiddlers: Musical program.

Refreshments

Hobo Feast: Hot dogs and coffee or hot chocolate.

A HALLOWEEN CAMPFIRE

Guests are notified to meet at some central point dressed for a hike. No one knows the route except the leaders. There are surprises at certain points. Finally the group comes upon a campfire. Here a ghost announces a nut hunt. Peanuts are hidden all about.

The group is then led to a second campfire, where a nearby tree is decorated with sacks containing bacon, wieners, buns, eggs, and pickles. Coffee is prepared over the campfire. Songs, jokes, and stunts are enjoyed. As the fire dies down, marshmallows can be roasted.

WITCH PARTY

Invitations—Black cardboard cats or bats can have the following invitation written on them in white ink.

"THE OLD WITCH WILL GET YOU IF YOU DON'T SHOW UP AT THE WITCH PARTY." "DID YOU SAY WITCH PARTY?" "YEAH, WITCH PARTY."
>   (date, time, and place)

Program

Giant Witch: A giant witch greets each guest just outside the door. The giant effect is achieved by having a person stand on a chair. Flowing robes cover the chair and lead to the floor. This witch simply motions the guests to enter.

Witch Greeter: If possible the group should be sent through a dark passageway, at the end of which an old witch stands with hand extended. Each person is required to shake hands. The witch's arm and hand are artificial, the latter being a glove stuffed with cold wet sand.

Witches' Graveyard: The guests are led into another dimly lighted room. One side of the room is decorated with what appear to be tombstones. These may be made by dropping white pillow cases over children's chairs. A witch explains to the group:

> Many a witch once young and gay
> Has passed along Death Valley's way.
> Their restless spirits roam and rave;
> Their bodies lie in the cold, cold grave.
>
> Just now we'd like to hear from you
> Some epitaphs you think will do,
> Or some you've seen, or some you've heard,
> When you are ready, you just say the word.

It might be well to have some persons primed with some good humorous epitaphs:

> Here lies the body of Susan Proctor,
> She died before they could get a doctor.
>
> Here lies the body of Sally Lonn,
> Her motor stopped but Sal went on.
>
> Here lies the body of Hattie Howe,
> She lied in life, she's lying now.
>
> Here lies the body of Johnny Bray,
> Who died maintaining his right of way;
> He was right, dead right, as he sped along;
> But he's just as dead as if he'd been dead wrong.
>
> Here lies the body of Bobby Bains,
> The road was slick, he had no chains.

Whodunit: The witch now announces that a "murder" is to be committed on the spot. Each person draws a slip of paper from a box. Only one slip is marked and it carries the word *murderer*. The lights are turned out and the group mills around the room until the "murderer" selects a victim by putting the hands loosely about someone's throat. That person screams (the more blood-curdling, the better), and falls to the floor. The lights are turned on. The prosecuting attorney, who has been previously selected, requires every person to take the witness stand. Each person except the guilty party must answer truthfully any question asked by the attorney. When the questioning is finished, the guests vote to decide on the guilty party. Then the murderer confesses. A good prosecuting attorney can make this a most interesting feature.

Witches' Den: The witches' den is a booth made of cornstalks. Guests are allowed to visit one at a time. Inside is an old witch who reads palms or uses some other fortunetelling device.

Witches' Paradise: The lights in this room should be covered with blue paper, or blue spotlights may be used. The room is decorated with corn shocks, pumpkins, hanging black cats and bats, stick candy and apples hanging by strings. Persons are allowed to help themselves to the apples and candy if they can get them without using their hands.

Witches' Race: Guests straddle broomsticks and race the length of the room and back.

Shadow Shows: The crowd is divided into two or more groups and each group presents a shadow show. All arrangements have been made for this by putting up a sheet, behind which they place a light at the proper distance to throw picture shadows on the sheet. Suggestions for shadow-show stunts:

Operation. A patient is brought in and put on a table. A nurse puts a large funnel over the patient's face. The patient slowly "loses consciousness." The doctor gets the tools ready—a saw, a hatchet, butcher knife, and various other implements. The doctor begins to work with the knife while the patient groans. A string of wieners, a toy dog ("hot dog"), and various other things are lifted out. Then the doctor begins to saw off a leg. The sound of the saw can be heard as it cuts through wood. In a moment part of the leg with a shoe on it is lifted up. This is achieved by having a stuffed leg ready. All this looks extremely funny in shadow pictures.

Ghost Stories: Have one or two good storytellers tell some thrilling ghost stories. Lights low for this feature.

Refreshments—Witches' punch and cake.

A PARTY FOR HALLOWEEN

Invitations

>The Black Cat bids you come
>   Next ——— eve at eight,
>Unto his mistress' home,
>   Prepared to stay quite late.
>Your fortune will be told,
>   Perhaps you'll get the ring;
>And please do bring some stunt
>   To speak or act or sing.
>(date and time)   (place)

These are written on white paper, folded, and hung on the neck of a black cat cut out of cardboard.

Decorations—Decorations may consist of bare branches, corn shocks, pumpkins, autumn leaves, moss. To secure a weird effect, hang gray crepe paper cut in strips between lights or at intervals around the room, with a lighted pumpkin placed here and there. All lights should be dim.

Little paper horns make attractive little witches for place cards. Dress up the horn in a full skirt, make arms of wire, make a broom from a toothpick and straw.

Program

Masks: A Halloween party is always more successful if the guests are masked for at least part of the evening.

Since it is often difficult to have guests come masked, why not have them make their masks after they arrive? This can easily be done by giving each guest a large paper sack and some colored pens or crayons. Cut out holes for the eyes. After all masks have been completed, the lights should be turned out. Each guest then puts on the sack and moves to a different position. When the lights are turned on again, each guest tries to identify as many people as possible. As each person is identified, a mark is put on his or her mask. As a surprise finish, give a prize to the guest who has the most marks, for being so well known.

Skull Ball: Guests sit or stand in a circle. One of the players is the witch and stands in the center. Someone in the circle has a ball painted to look like a skull. At the signal the skull is passed rapidly around or across the circle. If the one in the center catches the ball while it is in the air, the person who threw it becomes the witch and goes to the center. If the witch can touch the skull while it is still in some player's hand, that player becomes the witch.

Witch Hunt: Cut a number of cats, bats, and owls out of cardboard and hide them around the room before the party. The players march around in a circle while music is played. When the music stops the players find as many cats, bats, and owls as they can. When the music begins again, all must stop hunting and march until the music stops again. The game continues until all cut-outs have been found. Cats count one point, bats count three points, owls count five points. The person having the most points wins.

Retrieving the Witch's Broomstick: A small pumpkin is placed in the center of the floor. The players are divided into two equal sides and are numbered. The leader calls a number and the players from each side who have that number come to the front. These players are stationed at an equal distance from the pumpkin, holding a broomstick between them. At the signal, both pull, and the player who pulls the opponent past the pumpkin wins. The game continues until all have tried.

Bats, Goblins, and Elves: The players are divided into two equal sides at opposite ends of the room. Each team sends a player to the center. These are the Elves. Members of one team are Bats, the other, Goblins. The Elves call, "Bats change," and all Bats run to the opposite side of the room. The Elves catch all they can. Those caught stay and help. With "Goblins change," the game continues. At the end of four or five minutes, the side having the most players left wins.

Game of the Three Fates: Guests sit in a circle. Three Fates are chosen. The first whispers to each person in turn the name of his or her future sweetheart. The second Fate follows, whispering where the person will meet the sweetheart, as, "You will meet on a load of hay." The third Fate reveals the future: "You will be separated for many years by a quarrel, but will finally marry." Each guest must remember what is said by the Fates and each in turn must repeat the fortune. For example: "My future sweetheart's name is Obednego. We will meet next week and be married on a moonlight excursion."

Refreshments—Doughnuts, punch and apples; or, on a cold night, wieners and buns with coffee or hot chocolate.

A HALLOWEEN HIKE

If you live where an old fort, tower, lighthouse, or old church is available, an interesting Halloween hike could be planned. Arrange for all sorts of surprises along the way and at the destination—ghosts, weird noises, and the like. At the party, play Who Am I? requiring that all characters selected be dead. A good ghost story would furnish a fitting climax.

Refreshments—Hot chocolate and Brownies*.

HAUNTED HOUSE PARTY

Locate a house in another part of town. None but the leader should know its location. Decorate it with the usual black cats, streamers, candies, etc. The meeting place could be the church. Ask guests to come in costumes of some kind. Give no instructions, but bundle them into cars and tell them to follow their leader.

A circuitous route is followed through strange streets, turning many corners and through dark alleys till finally they draw up at a large residence in total darkness. They are met by a ghost who, with pointed finger, directs them through a tangle of bushes, tall grass, and low-hanging trees, till they come to a dark and forbidding cellar door, surmounted by a blinking skull. Abandon All Hope, reads a sign in luminous paint over the door. A chorus of groans and moans issue from the cellar. Guests are directed down the steps by the ghost and told to "follow the rope." Inside all is pitch dark. When they turn a corner, there suddenly appears before them a luminous skeleton.

Suddenly the skeleton raises its arms and starts toward them. A loud scream is heard, but strange hands pull them away from the grasp of the specter. On all sides one can see other skeletons, large and small, dancing up and down and screaming. It is truly a dream of the lower regions.

The screams and groans die out as they turn another corner and behold a man lying in a coffin. A ghastly green light in the coffin lid lights up his features in a truly gruesome manner. The dead man opens his eyes and, without warning, raises up in his coffin.

The rope trail leads through the cellar, up through the kitchen and then to the dressing rooms. In the darkened kitchen a noise is produced by allowing a small stream of water to fall into a metal tub.

Near the dressing rooms, a draped ghost directs the boys to one room, girls to another. Here they regain their scattered senses in the dismal room with grinning skulls over each light. Everyone then assembles in the main room, where the usual Halloween games are played. Then it's time for a stunt.

Beheading of the Ghosts: The victims are led, one by one, into the death chamber where a boy dressed as a devil carries a huge cardboard axe over his shoulder. Each guest is led by a ghost to a wooden block and made to kneel before it with the neck across it. The axman then raises his axe and as it descends, apparently on the victim's neck, the lights are extinguished and a resounding whack is heard, followed by a scream. When the lights are again turned on, the victim is gone and the axman stands waiting for the next victim. (The assistant had struck a heavy block of wood with a real axe and then pulled the victim away before the lights were again turned on.) This stunt should be done in full view of the rest of the crowd, while the assistant hides behind a curtain.

Have a ghost story told at exactly midnight. Everyone should sit in a circle on the floor while a burning pan of alcohol (to which salt has been added) is placed in the middle. Let a witch tell a story and time it so the alcohol burns out just at the most exciting part of the story. Have several luminous skeletons walk around the room dragging chairs behind them.

The luminous skeleton idea is very simple. Secure a picture of a skeleton, block it off into squares and then enlarge it to life size, drawing it on sign-painters cloth. This may also be done by enlarging a slide to life size and drawing it off. Paint over the lines with luminous paint, which can be bought at art or paint stores. Then cut off the arms, legs, and head, and pin it to the clothes of the person who is to take the part. Now expose the skeleton to a strong electric light for about ten minutes. In the dark this figure will now stand out like purple fire and remain luminous for about half an hour. One of the arms should be detached from the body and float around, approaching people, then dodging off in the distance. Many stunts will suggest themselves when these skeletons are finished. Small skeletons with movable arms and legs can be secured. Paint these the same way the larger figures were painted.

To make the dead man in the coffin, place a man on a table and lay cardboard boxes over him, cut and formed to resemble a coffin. Cover the boxes with black crepe paper, place two green bulbs inside near the face, and you will have a coffin fit for any ghost. The room should be in total darkness, therefore the lower part of the coffin need not be made since it cannot be seen.

HALLOWEEN SUGGESTIONS

Walnut Boats: Open a number of English walnuts, remove the meat, and in each half shell, fasten short pieces of different-colored Christmas candles. Each boat is named for a member of the party, and, after lighting, set afloat in a large pan or tub of water.

The behavior of these tiny boats will reveal the future of the people for whom they are named. Two may glide on together as if talking to each other, while one may be left alone—out in the cold. Again, two may start off and all the rest may follow in close pursuit. The one whose candle goes out first is destined to be an old bachelor or old maid.

What's Your Fate? Blindfolded players walk through a doorway in which are hung, a few inches apart, various objects: a candy heart, a thimble, an irregularly shaped stone, a toy truck. As the blindfolded person approaches the doorway, both hands must be extended, and the object first touched will indicate the person's future—the candy heart, a new girl or boy friend; the rough stone, a hard road to travel, etc. It will be easy to supply the ten or twelve different objects needed.

Saucers: Seven tiny saucers, each containing a different article, are presided over by a gypsy. The seeker is

blindfolded and touches one of the saucers. The contents of
the saucer tell the fortune:

Moss: A life of luxury. Money and worldly goods.
Thorn: Unhappy love. Disappointment.
Red Cloth: Military profession.
Blue Cloth: Navy for profession.
Forked Stick: Widow or widower.
Clear Water: Single blessedness.

A HALLOWEEN HARD-TIMES PARTY

Decorations—Cornstalks, jack-o'-lanterns made of cardboard boxes. Each guest is asked to come dressed in the
most dilapidated costume available.

Hard-luck Experiences: Guests must greet one another
with hard-luck experiences, such as: "I need 17 cents more
to have enough to pay my bus fare home where I have a sick
child (wife, husband, mother)," etc.

Bobbing for Apples: Interest could be added to this old
favorite by placing a penny in one apple, a thimble in
another, and a ring in another. The penny will prophesy
wealth; the thimble, single life; the ring, marriage within
the year.

Spiderweb Fortune: Draw a large spiderweb on smooth
yellow paper. In each section, write some fortune. Players
spin a top. The space on which the top stops indicates the
fortune.

Hoop Fortunes: A barrel hoop or hula hoop, stick candy,
slices of bread, red peppers, small candles, and strong cords
are needed. Cut the cord into different lengths and tie the
articles on the hoop. Suspend the hoop from the ceiling or
chandelier. Twist the cords holding it and spin it
merry-go-round fashion. Then the bite tells, for each guest,
in turn, endeavors to grasp one of the articles with the
teeth. If the guest bites candy, sweet and rosy is the future.

Bread portends plenty to eat, but an even, humdrum existence. The red pepper foretells trouble and a "hot time" generally. The candle indicates a short honeymoon.

Flame Fortunes: Fortunes are written on paper, wrapped in foil, and placed in a plate of alcohol. The alcohol is lighted and guests snatch a fortune from the flaming dish.

Apple Fortunes: After ducking for apples, each person breaks or cuts an apple in half, and counts the fortune in this fashion: one seed, disappointment in love; 2, early marriage; 3, legacy; 4, wealth; 5, a voyage; 6, fame; 7, attainment of one's most cherished wish. If there are more than seven seeds, the count goes back to number one.

Following this, stick two of the seeds on the forehead. The one that sticks longest indicates the fortune. The player can name them for two persons to decide which will be his or her mate, or call one *riches,* the other *poverty,* or one *get my wish,* the other *don't get my wish,* etc.

Poorhouse: Place chairs in a circle facing toward the center. Leave four openings, each three or four chair spaces wide. There should be chairs for all but two players. For the two left over, there are two chairs in the center of the circle. The players seated there are in the "poorhouse." As the music plays, all guests except the two in the poorhouse march on the outside of the chairs. At the signal, they all rush inside the circle and try to get chairs. The poorhouse couple also try to get seats in the circle. The two players left out take the seats in the poorhouse and the game proceeds. Players are allowed to enter the circle only through the original openings. It is illegal to step over the chairs or to move a chair. If desired, chairs may be arranged in twos and players may be required to play as couples, holding hands.

Canned Beans: Nail five tin cans to a board—one in each corner and one in the center. Give each player five tosses with a beanbag. Center can counts 25; top cans, 10 each; bottom cans, 5 each.

Refreshments

Hard-times Food: Sandwiches wrapped in newspaper; coffee or hot chocolate.

NOVEMBER

A U-SHARIT PARTY

Everyone is requested to bring at least one game or an idea for one. The game is explained to the crowd, and the person suggesting it may lead in playing it. If desired, someone else may lead the crowd in playing the games. Some people don't mind telling about a game, but they would be embarrassed if asked to direct a crowd in playing.

In a large crowd it would be impossible to play all the games suggested. Therefore it might be necessary to divide into four or more groups, with a leader for each group. These groups meet and each will plan for fifteen minutes or more of the program. Each person in the group suggests a game and the group decides which games to use. Let the groups vie with one another to see which can furnish the best entertainment. Video games may be used if enough television sets are available.

Groups draw for their order in the program. This drawing may be done by leaders of the groups, so that each group can better arrange its part of the program.

If the leader thinks there is any chance that suitable games may not be suggested, it might be well to have a preliminary meeting of the leaders to map out plans in case the groups should fall down in game ideas. Often a suggestion from the leader of a group will start the individuals making suggestions.

All those invited to the party may be urged to look up a game in a recreation book. If the church has a recreation library, put the books where they will be easily available.

Refreshments—Each person may be asked to bring some refreshments, with a limit being placed on the expenditure. All the food can be placed on a table, with guests choosing either their own, or that brought by someone else, potluck style. Or, make girls responsible for preparing and serving cake, while boys are responsible for ordering and serving ice cream or Eskimo pies.

A KNOXEM COLLEGE FOOTBALL PARTY

Invitations—Use yellow cardboard or paper footballs.

You are requested to report for football practice at _____ on Friday evening, November ____. No excuses accepted.
Signed: Athletic Committee, Knoxem College.

Decorations—Have a fake tackling dummy rigged up in one corner of the room. Use a lot of Knoxem College pennants made of crepe paper. Post slogans around the room. Suggestions:

A strong line aids a weak plunger. What's your line?
Tackle low, but don't dig up our grass.
Many a full-back is seen on sun-tan days.
They shall not pass.
Pass the ball—don't pass the buck.
A straight arm gaineth more ground than a crooked character.
Be sure all your sidestepping is done within bounds.

Program

Testing of Wind: Paper-sack-burst relay, or blow up balloons until they burst.

Falling on the Ball: Use beanbag on a piano stool. Players line up in equal sides. Each player is numbered. Leader calls a number and the two players with that number rush out to get possession of the beanbag. If a player can get back to the line with the beanbag without being tagged by the opponent, two points are scored. If a player is tagged, opponent scores one point.

Forward Passing: Two long lines of players. Pass toy balloons overhead down the lines. End player, upon receiving, runs to head of line and passes down again. This is continued until original head players are at the head of their lines.

Interference: Select about six couples. Tie toy balloons to the ankles of the girls, with strings twelve to eighteen inches long. Each girl links arms with her partner. At the signal, the battle is on. Each boy endeavors to protect his partner's balloon, while at the same time trying to burst the balloons of the opponents by stamping on them. Fast and furious for a few moments.

Signals: All players are seated in a circle. They number off, and players must remember their own numbers. A center player also takes a number. This player is IT and proceeds to call signals, calling from four to six numbers. No one moves until IT yells "Hike." Then all players whose numbers are called must find other seats. IT tries to get a seat in the grand rush. The player left out is IT for the new turn.

Refreshments—Hot apple cider and ham biscuits.

SUGGESTIONS FOR A THANKSGIVING PARTY

Thanks: For a group of thirty-six, write the word *thanks* six times. Cut these into single letters and give each person one letter. Then tell guests they are to find enough people to spell the word *thanks*. As they discover players with the letters they want, they link arms and search for others until the word is spelled. This goes on until all persons have found a group. Some award may be given to the first group to spell the word. No player can link arms with players other than those who have the letter immediately preceding or following theirs in the word *thanks.*

Shouting Proverbs: Each group of six now decides on some proverb of six words, such as, A stitch in time saves nine. Each player is assigned one word in this proverb. The leader counts "One, Two, Three," and all players in the group of six shout their words at the same time. The other groups try to guess what proverb has been shouted. Try it over until some group guesses it or they all give up. Then another group shouts its proverb: All that glitters is not gold, or, Make hay while the sun shines.

Thanksgiving: Each person is given a piece of paper and told to form as many words as possible from the word *Thanksgiving.* Proper names are excluded. Give about five minutes for this and then let players count their own lists. Have the winner read the list.

Turkey or Thanks: Make as many sets of cubes as you will need for Progressive Turkey. Some lumber yard or carpenter shop can make these for you. Six cubes will be necessary for a set. On the six sides of each cube write the letters (with pencil, crayon, or ink) of the word *turkey,* one letter to a side. The word *thanks* may be used in the same manner.

For thirty-six people, nine sets of cubes will be necessary.

Four players to a table. Each player tosses the six cubes out on the table. If the cubes show T and H, the player scores 5 points. If THA, 10 points; THAN, 15; THANK, 20; THANKS, 25, plus 10 for getting them all. Any player throwing three Ts cancels his or her entire score up to that time. The two winners at each table should progress to the next table. Players keep their scores and the two ending the evening with the largest scores are declared winners.

Refreshments—Turkey-salad sandwiches and hot tea.

DECEMBER

A CHRISTMAS PARTY

Invitations—Cut tiny green Christmas trees from construction paper. The invitation may be written on a slip of paper and passed through two slits in the tree. Ask guests to bring a gift costing no more than one dollar and wrapped in Christmas paper.

Program

Christmas Caps: Divide your crowd into two groups. Give one group red crepe paper, the other green. Tape, pins, and string should also be furnished. The paper can be cut in strips large enough to fit about the head. Each group is given ten minutes to make caps to wear. At the end of that time they parade before the judges' stand. The judges decide which group best expresses beauty and originality in its headgear. An award may be also made to the individual with the most clever creation. These caps are to be worn throughout the evening.

Christmas Bell Trade: Each player is provided with a tiny paper bell. One player is given a gold bell; all the rest are red. Players walk about with closed hands and introduce themselves to other players. As they do so they extend their clenched hands and tap one of the extended hands of the other players. If the player tapped happens to have his or her bell in the hand tapped that player must trade with the other player. At the end of three minutes the leader blows a whistle and the player holding the gold bell is given a large stick of candy as a prize.

Telegrams to Santa: Each couple is given three minutes to write a telegram to Santa Claus, using, in order, the letters S-A-N-T-A C-L-A-U-S. In small crowds these telegrams may be read and the best decided by vote. The winning couple may be given two small dishes of ice cream, and two spoons tied together with a piece of string about six inches long. They must eat the ice cream without untying the spoons.

When the crowd is large it would be best to let the Green Caps contest against the Red Caps. Each side could write three telegrams. Judges would decide on the best.

Gift Exchange: All players stand in a circle, and as the music plays, the gifts they brought are passed around the circle to the right. When the music stops each package is kept by the player who happens to have it at that time. The player unwraps it and, after seeing what it is, if not satisfied, may rewrap it and endeavor to swap with some other player. Players try to disguise the nature of the gift by the way it is wrapped. There is a time limit of ten minutes on the swapping period. At the end of that time, players must keep the presents they have.

Christmas Swipe: A large sack containing candies and trinkets of various sorts is hung in the center of the room. Players from the Red Caps and Green Caps, in turn, are blindfolded, turned about, and given an opportunity to bring the sack down with one swipe of a wand. If a Red Cap brings down the sack, then that team is privileged to scramble for the contents. If it is brought down by a Green Cap, then only the Greens have that privilege. Players are not allowed to coach a contestant.

Christmas Present Relay: From four to ten players represent each side. Players must run to a chair or table, untie, unwrap, rewrap, and retie a Christmas package.

They then run back and touch off the next teammate. Have extra tape and ribbon available.

Christmas Stocking Contest: Two or more red stockings are hung, the number depending on the number of contestants on each side. Each contestant is provided with a teaspoon and three apples. These apples must be picked off the floor with the spoon, carried to the stocking, and dropped in. This game may be run as a relay, each runner putting in just one apple, returning and handing the spoon to the next runner. The apples must be put into the stocking without the aid of the extra hand.

Christmas Trail: Each player selects a string from a mass of strings in one corner of the room. This string is then followed to the end. It passes along the floor and is tangled and tied with strings of other players. It is wound around chair legs, posts, etc. It may lead upstairs and back. When the end is reached, a sack containing candies and fruit, or some sort of noise-making toy may be found. The players then form a line and march about the room playing their instruments. The color of the girls' strings and that of the boys may be different. Partners for refreshments could be matched by tying the ends of strings together.

Refreshments—Cherry pie and warm beverage.

A SANTA CLAUS PARTY

This party can be given for either a large or small group. Ask each guest to bring an inexpensive wrapped gift, cost limited to one dollar.

Pinning on Santa's Pack: The old game of pinning the tail on the donkey, adapted. The person who pins the pack most accurately receives a prize. Guests should try this as they arrive at the party.

Debate: Resolved—That There Ain't No Santa Claus. Have one or two speakers on each side. Appoint the debaters a week or so in advance. Limit speeches to five minutes.

Santa's Pack: Give each player the name of a certain thing that might be in Santa's pack—doll, horn, knife, candy, orange, truck, gun, tie, etc. The crowd is seated in a circle with no vacant chairs. The player who is without a chair walks around the circle, telling a story about Santa filling up his pack before starting on his journey. "He put in a pretty little doll, a Scout knife," etc. As the articles are mentioned, the people bearing those names get up and follow the player around the circle, placing their hands on the shoulders of the person immediately preceding. When the player who is telling the story says "Reindeer," each player makes an effort to get a chair, the storyteller among them. The player left without a chair starts another story, and the game continues.

Santa Claus Letters: Each person is given pencil and paper and asked to write a Santa Claus letter for the player on the right. If the crowd is small, each player then reads the letter. If the crowd is large, the letters are collected and a committee selects those to be read to the group.

Santa's Bag of Stunts: Write certain stunts on slips of paper. Put them in a sack and have each player draw one to perform.

1. Select a partner and pose for one of those old-time photographs, the girl sitting and the boy standing beside her, hat held stiffly across the chest.

2. Propose to anyone of the opposite sex in the room, just to show how it is done.

3. Sing in three keys—a low HO HO HO! then middle register Ha Ha Ha! then a high Hee Hee Hee!

4. Pantomime a baseball player striking out—swinging on the first two, then having the third strike called by the umpire.

5. Dramatize the actions and expressions of a small boy at an exciting wild west show.

6. Pantomime the actions and expression of a teenage girl at a romantic movie.

7. Give your own explanation of how the custom of allowing a woman to precede a man on entering a door originated.

8. Briefly state three reasons why you think men are superior to women, whether you believe what you are saying or not.

9. Briefly state three reasons why you think women are superior to men, whether you believe what you are saying or not.

10. Dramatize rocking a baby to sleep.

Santa's Gifts: The gifts brought by the guests were collected upon arrival and numbered in consecutive order. Each player draws a number from a hat. The packages are given to Santa and he calls the numbers written on them. The player wth the number called gets the package. If players are not satisfied, they may trade.

Refreshments—Christmas Tree Salad* and hot Russian Tea*.

A CHRISTMAS CAROL FESTIVAL

Christmas caroling was widely popular in the Middle Ages, being especially associated with English traditions. In 1525 we find a specific prohibition entered against "carols, bells, and merrymaking" because of the illness of King Henry VIII. To this day it is the custom in England for troops of men and boys to go about the villages several nights before Christmas, singing carols.

In America, too, caroling is a feature of the Christmas season in many cities and towns. Usually the groups go out on Christmas Eve and sing wherever a lighted candle appears in the window. It is a beautiful custom and worthy of perpetuation.

Program

Sing: "Joy to the World."

Read: Luke 2:8-20.

Sing: "There's a Song in the Air."

Read: A Christmas story—"The First Christmas Tree," by Van Dyke.

"Silent Night": While a hidden quartet sings this beautiful Christmas song, present tableaux on the platform. For the first verse, the manger and Mary. For the second verse, shepherds assume reverent attitude before the manger. On the third verse, a lighted cross appears at the back of the platform; Mary and shepherds kneel, facing the cross.

Sing: "Hark, the Herald Angels Sing."

Present: A short Christmas play or the dramatization of another carol.

Sing: "O Come All Ye Faithful."

Christmas Greetings: Each person is given a card with a sprig of holly attached. Allow ten minutes for guests to obtain as many Christmas greetings as possible on the card, from others in the group. An award is made to the one who gets the most. All greetings will be the same—"Merry Christmas," with the initials of the writer.

Illustrated Christmas Gifts: Have the crowd pair off in couples. Arrange chairs in two rows, back to back. Partners are seated with their backs to each other. Each couple is furnished pencil and paper. One partner describes some Christmas gift, without naming the gift. The other tries to draw what is described. The one giving the description must not look until the leader calls time. The name of the article described is written beneath the drawing, and the works of art are passed around for inspection. Give ten minutes for the artists to work.

Human Christmas Trees: Guests were asked to bring some toy or trinket, not to cost over one dollar. As guests arrived their presents were collected, names were placed on them, and they were turned over to the tree-decorating committees.

Have three or four persons act as trees. They wear tight-fitting green crepe-paper caps, with red tassels on top, and are placed at a sufficient distance from one another to allow the groups space in which to work. The crowd is divided into as many groups as there are "trees." Each tree is numbered. The players draw numbers, then gather about their trees. Tinsel, garlands, popcorn, needle and thread, etc., are provided. The trees are then decorated and presents are hung on them or placed about the foot of the tree. When the job is finished the trees are put on display. Allow fifteen or twenty minutes for decoration of the trees.

Then the leader announces that guests are to find the trees which hold their presents and help themselves. Presents are provided for all. A parade following the distribution of gifts would be quite interesting, especially if some noise-making toys have been provided.

Have the crowd sing one verse of "Hark, the Herald Angels Sing" before singing a verse of "Silent Night" as the closing carol.

Refreshments—Party Cheese Ball* and crackers; White Fruitcake*, punch.

OTHER CHRISTMAS SUGGESTIONS

Bridgeboard: On one edge of a large sheet of cardboard, cut out a series of arches large enough to admit a small ball. Number each arch: 5, 10, etc. Tape or tack this cardboard in a doorway so that the arches rest on the floor. Players try to roll a ball through the numbered arches. One person is appointed to act as scorekeeper, to record the number of the arch through which each ball rolls; another is in the next room to return balls sent through the arches. The player with the largest count wins.

Safety Stars: Stretch a piece of paper about five feet high around the walls of the room. On it, at different heights and places, paste large stars. The players march slowly around the room to music, not being allowed to touch the wall. When the music stops, every player must have a hand on a star. The players left without stars are given seats in the center of the room and that many stars are taken down from the wall. This is repeated until only one star is left to be contested for by two or more players.

Rompiendo la Piñata: This is a Mexican Christmas game. A large paper bag is filled with nuts and candy, each piece wrapped. The mouth of the bag is tied and the bag is hung from the ceiling with a cord. The bag is painted to represent a person or an animal, or may be decorated with various designs.

The guests, each in turn, are given a stick and, blindfolded, try to break the piñata. Only one stroke is allowed, and the player is not permitted to grope for the bag. When someone finally breaks the bag and the contents are scattered, the players scramble for them.

Sometimes a bit of novelty is introduced by preparing three piñatas—the first filled with flour and rice, the second with old shoes, the third with the sweets.

Hunting Christmas Presents: Guests are told that hidden about the room are Christmas presents, one for each person. Guests are not permitted to disturb a present intended for someone else, nor are they permitted to tell others where their packages are. Guests must hunt until each finds his or her own package.

Making Christmas Presents: Provide patterns for cardboard toys—a clown, a horse, a teddy bear, a Santa Claus. If the toys can be made to move by pulling a string, so much the better. Each guest has been asked to bring cardboard (a suit box or hat box or heavier material if possible), scissors, crayons or colored pens, pencil, an old razor blade, and cotton. The committee should have on hand brads, paste, and tape. Lots of fun can be had making these toys. There will be some in the group who will do a very artistic job. Perhaps the toys can be taken to a children's hospital. A shadow show could be put on with some of the articles made.

A Letter to Santa Claus: Have a copy of this letter and a pencil ready for each guest. Have guests complete the letters. Read the letters aloud to see whether guests can guess who wrote them; if not, read the names signed to the letters.

Dear Santa,

Thought I'd better take time out of my busy schedule and drop you a line. My Christmas shopping is _____ finished.
                        (not, almost, all)

Every year I seem to receive a _____ .

I really wish you would bring me a _____ .

The most exciting Christmas gift I ever received was a _____

_____ .

Here are some facts you might like to know about me to make your Christmas shopping easier:

My favorite color: _____

My favorite TV program: _____

My pet peeves: _____

My favorite dessert: _____

Public figure I admire most: _____

_____

Homework (housework) I like most: _____

_____

Homework (housework) I like least: _____

_____

Well, so long for now, Santa! See you December 25!
Yours truly,

Ima Yule Tide

The Night Before Christmas: Ask members of the group for suggestions to fill in the blanks in the following story. Do not let them know what you are doing. Ask for "period of time," "holiday," "building," etc. After all the blanks are filled in, read the story aloud to the group.

'Twas the _____ before _____ ,
    (period of time)   (holiday)

when all through the _____
                              (building)

Not a creature was stirring, not even a _____ ;
                                            (animal)

The _____ were hung by the chimney with care,
    (wearing apparel)

In hopes that _____ soon would be there;
                (famous character)

The children were nestled all snug in their _____,
                                            (furniture)

While visions of _____ danced in their _____;
                  (food)   (part of body)

And _____ in her kerchief,
              (female relative)

   and I in my _____,
                              (wearing apparel)

Had just settled our brains for a long winter's nap,

When out on the lawn there arose such a clatter,

I _____ from the _____
        (action verb)   (furniture)

   to see what was the matter.

Away to the window I flew like a flash,

Tore open the shutters and threw up the sash.

The _____ on the breast of the new-fallen snow
         (planet)

Gave the luster of mid-day to objects below,

When, what to my wondering _____ should appear,
                            (part of body)

But a miniature _____ , and eight tiny _____ ,
                  (vehicle)   (animal)

With a little old driver, so lively and _____ ,
                                          (adjective)

I knew in a moment it must be _____ .
                                    (famous character)

More rapid than _____ his coursers they came,
                        (bird)

And he whistled, and shouted, and called them by name;

"Now, _____ ! now, _____ ! now, _____ and _____ !
      (name)   (name)   (name)   (name)

On, _____ ! on, _____ ! on, _____ and _____ !
    (name)   (name)   (name)   (name)

To the top of the porch! To the top of the wall!

Now dash away! dash away! dash away all!" . . .

So up to the house-top the coursers they flew,

With the sleigh full of toys, and _____, too.
                                      (famous character)

And then, in a twinkling, I heard on the roof

The prancing and pawing of each little hoof.

As I drew in my head, and was turning around,

Down the chimney _____ came with a bound.
                      (famous character)

He was dressed all in fur, from his head to his foot,

And his clothes were all tarnished with ashes and soot;

A bundle of _____ he had flung on his back,
                 (noun)

And he looked like a peddler just opening his pack.

His _____ —how they twinkled!
              (part of body)

his _____ how merry!
              (part of body)

His cheeks were like _____, his nose like a _____!
                        (flower)   (fruit)

His droll little mouth was drawn up like a bow,

And the beard of his chin was as _____ as the snow;
                                    (color)

The stump of a pipe he held tight in his teeth,

And the smoke it encircled his head like a wreath;

He had a broad _____ and a little round _____,
                (part of body)   (part of body)

That shook, when he laughed, like a bowlful of _____ .
                                                    (food)

He was chubby and _____, a right jolly old elf,
                        (adjective)

And I laughed when I saw him, in spite of myself;

A wink of his _____ and a twist of his _____,
                (part of body)   (part of body)

Soon gave me to know I had nothing to dread;

He spoke not a word, but went straight to his work,

And filled all the _____ ; then turned with a jerk,
                        (piece of clothing)

And laying his finger aside of his _____,
                                            (part of body)

And giving a nod, up the chimney he rose;

He _____ to his _____ ,
        (action verb)   (vehicle)

to his team gave a _____,
                              (sharp sound)

And away they all flew like the down of a thistle.

But I heard him exclaim, ere he drove out of sight,

"Happy Christmas to all, and to all a _____."
                                        (friendly greeting)

"A Visit from St. Nicholas," *Clement Clark Moore*

HORS D'OEUVRES AND SOUPS

PARTY CHEESE BALL

2 (8 oz.) pkgs. cream
  cheese, softened
1 T. pimiento, chopped
1 T. onion, finely chopped
1 tsp. lemon juice
Dash salt

2 cups sharp cheddar
  cheese, shredded
1 T. green pepper, chopped
2 tsp. Worcestershire sauce
Dash cayenne pepper
Pecans, finely chopped

Combine cheeses, mixing until well blended. Add other ingredients; mix well. Shape into ball; roll in chopped pecans.

CHEESE BALL

2 (8 oz.) pkgs. cream
  cheese, softened
1 jar dried beef, chopped
1 T. mayonnaise

1 bunch green onions,
  chopped
1 T. horseradish

Mix together and shape into ball.

CUCUMBER DIP

1 cucumber	1 small onion
1 stalk celery	1 green pepper

Chop all ingredients fine and drain. Soften 1 envelope unflavored gelatin in 3 T. water. Add 1 pint mayonnaise. Combine with chopped ingredients and mix well.

CHEESY WALNUT PINWHEELS

1 cup biscuit mix
¼ cup cheddar cheese, shredded
¼ cup cold water
¼ cup walnuts, finely chopped
1 (3 oz.) pkg. cream-cheese, softened
2 T. onion, finely chopped
1 T. mayonnaise

Mix biscuit mix and water until soft dough forms; beat 20 strokes. Gently smooth into ball on floured cloth-covered board. Knead 5 times. Roll into 12 X 9 inch rectangle. Mix remaining ingredients; spread evenly over dough to within ¼ inch of edges. Roll up tightly, beginning at 12-inch side. Seal well by pinching edge of dough into roll. Wrap and refrigerate until thoroughly chilled, at least 2 hours.

Heat oven to 400°. Cut roll into ¼-inch slices. Arrange slices cut sides down on greased cookie sheet. Bake until golden brown, 10 to 12 minutes. Makes 40 appetizers.

CLAM CHOWDER

1 pt. clams, chopped fine
3 slices salt pork
5 medium potatoes, cubed
1 medium onion, chopped fine

Fry salt pork until light brown. Add other ingredients and 1 quart water. Cook slowly about 1 to 1½ hours (no longer).

MAIN DISHES

PORK CHOP CASSEROLE

4 lean pork chops	4 T. canned tomatoes
4 T. uncooked rice	Salt and pepper
4 thick onion slices	

Place pork chops in baking dish and place 1 T. rice on top of each chop, then tomatoes and onion slices. Sprinkle with salt and pepper. Pour hot water up to top of chops. Cover and cook slowly 1½ hours in 375° oven.

BEEF AND CORN CASSEROLE

1 (8 oz.) box shell macaroni	1 (3 oz.) can chopped
2 lbs. ground beef	mushrooms
1 stick butter	½ cup ripe olives, chopped
2 medium onions, chopped	1 can tomatoes
1 green pepper, chopped	1 (8 oz.) can whole kernel
2 tsp. salt	corn
¼ tsp. pepper	2 cups cheese, grated
1 tsp. chili powder	1 T. Worcestershire sauce

Cook macaroni according to package directions. Drain. Brown meat in butter with onions and green pepper. Stir in other ingredients, then add macaroni. Toss together. Bake in 350° oven for 30 min.

CREAMED EGGS

5 hard-boiled eggs	2⅓ cups milk
5 T. butter	½ cup bread crumbs
5 T. flour	

Slice eggs. Melt butter and blend in flour. Add milk and stir over low heat until mixture boils. Place a layer of sliced eggs in well-greased casserole. Cover with sauce. Repeat till dish is filled. Sprinkle top with bread crumbs. Dot with butter. Heat in medium oven until warm. Serve at once.

SHRIMP CREOLE

1 cup onion, chopped   ½ cup green pepper,
¼ cup shortening   chopped

Sauté onion and green pepper in shortening. Add 1 can tomatoes and 1 small can tomato sauce, salt and pepper.

Add herb bouquet tied in a small cloth:

2 or 3 bay leaves   Thyme
Parsley flakes   Garlic
Onion salt

Add water to mixture if needed. Simmer and then add about 2 lbs. shrimp. Serve over rice. Serves 6.

STEW BEEF CASSEROLE

  1 lb. boneless stew beef, cut into small pieces
3 or 4 medium potatoes, sliced
1 or more carrots, sliced
1 medium onion, sliced
1 can cream of mushroom soup

Place beef in bottom of 2 qt. casserole. Add potatoes, carrots, and onions in layers. Add soup and salt and pepper to taste. Add garlic or any preferred seasoning. *Add no water.* Cover and bake at 275° for 3 hours.

CHICKEN CASSEROLE

6 chicken breasts   1 cup sour cream
2 cans cream of chicken   1 pkg. Ritz crackers,
  soup   crumbled
1 stick margarine

Cook chicken breasts, remove and cut up meat. Mix with sour cream and soup. Top with crumbled crackers. Melt margarine and pour over. Bake at 350° for 15 minutes.

TOMATO-SMOTHERED STEAK

1½ lbs. round steak
4 T. flour
1½ tsp. salt
½ tsp. pepper
3 T. shortening
1 medium onion, sliced
¼ cup celery, chopped
½ cup green pepper, chopped
1 (no. 2½) can tomatoes

Mix flour, ½ tsp. salt, and pepper. Pound one half of this mixture into steak. Brown slowly in shortening. Remove steak. Add onion, celery, and green pepper. Cook until onion is browned. Add rest of flour mixture and 1 tsp. salt. Stir to a paste. Add tomatoes. Pour sauce over meat and bake covered at 350° for 1½ hours.

PEPPER STEAK

Steak (cut in thin strips)
3 to 4 T. soy sauce
2 to 2½ cups water
1 bouillon cube
2 onions, sliced
2 green peppers, cut in rings
1 large can chow mein vegetables
3 T. cornstarch

Flour, salt, and pepper steak. Brown steak and add soy sauce, water, and bouillon cube. Cover and cook over low heat until tender.

Add onion and green pepper. Add chow mein vegetables. Mix cornstarch with enough water to make thin paste. Stir in. Serve over rice or chow mein noodles.

SCALLOPED TOMATOES

1 (no. 2½) can tomatoes
1 medium onion, chopped
¼ cup (or more) margarine
1¼ cup dried bread cubes
1 tsp. salt
⅛ tsp. pepper
½ cup brown sugar

Sauté onion in margarine. Add bread cubes; cook slowly. Stir in tomatoes; add seasonings. Place in buttered baking dish. Bake at 350° for 45 minutes.

BAKED MASHED POTATOES

1 lb. potatoes
2 eggs, separated
Salt

2 T. sour cream
1 T. butter

Cook and mash the potatoes. Add egg yolks, sour cream, and butter. Mix well. Beat egg whites and fold half into mashed potatoes. Spoon into baking dish and cover with rest of the egg whites. Bake in 350° oven until brown.

ASPARAGUS CASSEROLE

2 lbs. asparagus
2 T. green pepper, chopped
½ cup American cheese,
    grated

2 cups medium white sauce
6 hard-cooked eggs, sliced
¾ cup dried whole-wheat
    bread crumbs

Prepare asparagus and cut into small pieces. Arrange a layer in bottom of casserole. Cover with white sauce and a layer of eggs and sprinkle some cheese on the eggs. Repeat. Add bread crumbs last. Bake at 350° for 45 minutes.

CABBAGE CASSEROLE

1 medium head cabbage
1 large onion
Outside stalks of one
  bunch celery

White sauce
2 hard-boiled eggs, sliced
2 cups sharp cheese, grated

Boil cabbage, onion, and celery together until tender. Drain well and chop fine. Add eggs to white sauce. Place layer of cabbage in baking dish, then white sauce, then cheese. Repeat layers, with cheese layer last. Bake at 350° 30 minutes or until cheese is melted.

SALADS

CHRISTMAS TREE SALAD

1 pkg. lime-flavored gelatin
Fresh or canned fruit, chopped
Maraschino cherries, chopped

Make gelatin according to directions. When partly thickened, add fruit. Pour mixture into cone-shaped paper cups and place each cup in a glass. Refrigerate until firm. Unmold and serve pointed end up.

STRAWBERRY SALAD

2 small pkgs. strawberry
  gelatin
1 pkg. unflavored gelatin
1 cup hot water
2 cups cold water

3 bananas, mashed
1 cup crushed pineapple
1 (10 oz.) pkg. frozen
  strawberries
½ pt. sour cream

Mix together everything except sour cream. Pour half of mixture in 8-inch pan and refrigerate until thickened. (Keep other half over warm water.) Cover first half evenly with sour cream. Then pour remaining mixture over sour cream and chill until set.

GELATIN LIME SALAD

1 large pkg. lime gelatin 1 cup pecans, chopped
1 large pkg. cream cheese 1 can crushed pineapple

Mix cream cheese with gelatin (adding water as directed on box). Add pecans and pineapple. Chill. Garnish with small marshmallows.

RECEPTION SALAD

1 pkg. lemon gelatin
1 (no. 2) can crushed
 pineapple
½ cup celery, chopped
⅔ cup nuts, chopped

2 (3 oz.) pkgs. cream
 cheese, softened
1 (4 oz.) can pimientos
⅛ tsp. salt
⅔ large container of
 whipped topping

Mix cream cheese and pimientos. Drain pineapple. Dissolve gelatin in hot pineapple juice. Refrigerate. When it begins to thicken, mix in other ingredients, except topping. Fold in topping. Makes 1 large or 12 small molds. Serve on lettuce.

GELATIN DELIGHT

1 pkg. gelatin, any flavor
1 cup boiling water
½ cup cold water
1 (3 oz.) pkg. cream cheese
2 tsp. mayonnaise
½ cup sour cream

1 cup crushed pineapple
½ cup fruit cocktail
½ cup Mandarin oranges
½ cup cherries
1 cup whipped topping
1 cup marshmallows

Soften gelatin in hot water. Add cold water. Refrigerate until partly thickened. Add cream cheese, mayonnaise, and sour cream. Mix well with beater. Add all other ingredients and refrigerate until firm. Serve on lettuce.

SAWDUST SALAD

1 box orange gelatin	3 or 4 bananas, sliced
1 box lemon gelatin	1 can crushed pineapple
2 cups hot water	1 pkg. marshmallows
1¼ cups cold water	

Dissolve gelatin in hot water, add cold water. Drain pineapple (reserve juice). Add pineapple to bananas, and mix gelatin and fruit together. Place a layer of marshmallows on top of mixture. Place in refrigerator until firm.

2 eggs, well beaten	6 T. flour
1 cup sugar	2 cups pineapple juice (add water to make 2 cups)

Mix in order given. Cook until thick and let cool. Spread on top of gelatin & fruit mixture.

1 (8 oz.) pkg. cream cheese
1 large carton whipped topping

Mix cream cheese with topping. Spread over salad. Sprinkle with nuts or grated cheese. Makes a large salad or may be halved. Use a 3 qt. oblong pyrex dish for a big salad.

HEAVENLY HASH

2 apples, diced	1 large can pineapple
½ cup cherries, chopped	2 bananas, sliced
2 oranges, peeled and cut	½ cup pecans, chopped
2 cups small marshmallows	1 cup whipped cream or whipped topping

Mix fruit, nuts, and marshmallows. Stir in topping. Chill well before serving. Yields 10 to 12 servings.

FROZEN BANANA SALAD

This salad is very rich and sweet. Use it in place of dessert on a sweltering hot day to top off a light luncheon or supper. If used as a salad, serve small portions.

1 tsp. lemon juice	½ cup red cherries, halved
1 tsp. salt	½ cup pecans, chopped
4 T. mayonnaise	1 cup heavy cream,
2 pkgs. cream cheese,	whipped
softened	3 ripe bananas, cubed
4 T. crushed pineapple	

Add lemon juice and salt to mayonnaise and stir into cream cheese. Blend well. Add pineapple, cherries, and nuts. Fold in whipped cream. Lightly fold in bananas. Turn into refrigerator trays and freeze until firm, about 3 hours. Unmold. Cut into squares and serve on lettuce. Serves 6 to 8. Garnish with additional cherries, if desired.

FIVE CUP SALAD

1 cup crushed pineapple	1 cup dry flake coconut
1 cup fruit cocktail	1 cup sour cream
1 cup small marshmallows	Nuts and maraschino cherries, if desired

Mix ingredients and chill several hours or overnight.

CHICKEN SALAD

1 cup cooked chicken, cubed	¼ cup salted pecans, chopped
½ cup celery, diced	⅓ cup mayonnaise
½ cup crushed pineapple, well drained	½ jar stuffed olives

Combine ingredients and toss together lightly. Season with salt and pepper if desired. Serve on lettuce and garnish with stuffed olives. Serves 3 to 4.

CHICKEN SALAD

5 cups cooked chicken, cut in small chunks
2 T. salad oil
2 T. lemon juice
2 T. vinegar
1 tsp. salt

½ cups celery, diced
1 (3 oz.) can Mandarin orange sections, drained
1 cup toasted slivered almonds (optional)
1½ cups mayonnaise
6 hard-boiled eggs, sliced
1½ cups small green ripe grapes or sweet pickles

Combine chicken, oil, lemon juice, vinegar, and salt. Let stand while preparing remaining ingredients, or refrigerate mixture overnight. Then gently toss together all ingredients.

BREADS

ROLLS

1 pkg. dry yeast
1½ stick margarine
2 cups very warm water
6 cups self-rising unsifted flour

Mix yeast and water together and set aside. Melt margarine. Stir in yeast and add flour gradually. Do not beat. Fill greased muffin cups ⅔ full. Bake for 20 minutes at 350°.

REFRIGERATOR ROLLS

2 pkgs. yeast
2 eggs, beaten
1 cup lukewarm water
6 cups unsifted all-purpose flour (approximately)
1 cup shortening
½ cup sugar
1 T. salt
1 cup boiling water

Soften yeast in lukewarm water. Mix shortening, sugar, salt, and boiling water. When cooled to lukewarm, add softened yeast. Add eggs and mix well. Sift flour slowly into the mixture and beat well. Cover and refrigerate until chilled. Shape into rolls and let rise in warm place until double in bulk. Bake at 400° until golden brown.

These need not be placed in refrigerator unless they are to be kept for another day. You can let the dough rise, and then make into rolls. You can also punch the dough down if it rises too soon.

BANANA BREAD

½ cup shortening
½ cup nuts
1 cup sugar
2 cups all-purpose flour
1 cup ripe bananas, mashed
1 tsp. soda
2 eggs, beaten

Cream shortening and sugar. Blend in eggs and bananas. Stir in dry ingredients and nuts. Pour batter into greased loaf pan. Bake 55 to 60 minutes at 350°.

RIPPLE COFFEECAKE

1½ cups unsifted flour	1 cup sugar
1 tsp. baking powder	1 tsp. vanilla
½ tsp. baking soda	2 eggs
½ tsp. salt	8 oz. sour cream
½ cup butter	*Cocoa Filling*

Thoroughly stir together flour, baking powder, soda, and salt. Cream butter, sugar, and vanilla. Beat in eggs one at a time. Stir in flour mixture in 3 additions, alternately with sour cream, just until smooth. Spread ½ of batter in a 9 X 9 cake pan lined with wax paper on bottom. Sprinkle Cocoa Filling over batter; Add remaining batter. Bake in preheated 350° oven until it tests done, about 35 minutes. Let stand on wire rack 5 minutes; turn out.

Cocoa Filling— Stir together:

> 2 T. unsweetened cocoa
> ¼ cup sugar
> ⅓ cup finely chopped walnuts

TWO LOAVES OATMEAL BREAD

1 cup quick-cooking oatmeal	½ cup molasses
5 cups unsifted flour (white, or ½ white, ½ whole wheat)	2½ cups boiling water
	2 T. butter or margarine
	2 T. brown sugar
	2 pkgs. dry yeast

Pour boiling water over oatmeal. Add butter or margarine, brown sugar, and molasses. Mix well and let stand until lukewarm. Add flour and sprinkle yeast over mixture. Mix thoroughly. Let rise until double in bulk (keep in warm place and cover with cloth). Punch down and mix into a ball. Lift out onto floured board. Knead for 10 minutes (probably adding another cup flour while kneading). Place in two loaf pans. Let rise to top of pans. Bake at 400° for 20 minutes; reduce heat to 350° and bake 30 minutes.

CORN BREAD

1 cup corn meal	1 cup buttermilk
1 cup flour	
½ tsp. salt	If desired:
¼ tsp. soda	1 egg, beaten
1 scant tsp. baking powder	1 tsp. sugar

Mix well and bake in 425° oven 20 to 25 minutes.

COOKIES

BROWNIES

½ cup vegetable oil or melted butter	½ cup unsifted all-purpose flour
1 cup sugar	⅓ cup cocoa
1 tsp. vanilla	¼ tsp. baking powder
2 eggs	¼ tsp. salt
	½ cup chopped nuts (optional)

Blend oil, sugar, and vanilla. Add eggs and beat well. Combine flour, cocoa, baking powder, and salt; add gradually to egg mixture until well blended. Stir in nuts. Spread in greased 9-inch square pan. Bake at 350° for 20 to 25 minutes or until it begins to pull away from edge of pan. Cool in pan, frost if desired; cut into squares. Makes 16.

Creamy Brownie Frosting

3 T. butter	½ tsp. vanilla
3 T. cocoa	1 cup powdered sugar
1 T. light corn syrup or honey	1 or 2 T. milk

Cream butter, cocoa, corn syrup, and vanilla. Add sugar and milk; beat to spreading consistency. Makes about 1 cup.

PEANUT BLOSSOMS

1 cup granulated sugar
1 cup packed brown sugar
1 cup butter or margarine
1 cup creamy peanut
  butter
2 eggs
2 (10 oz.) pkgs. chocolate
  "kisses"

¼ cup milk
2 tsp. vanilla
3½ cups sifted all-purpose
  flour
2 tsp. baking soda
1 tsp. salt

Cream sugars, butter or margarine, and peanut butter. Beat in eggs, milk, and vanilla. Sift together flour, soda, and salt; stir into egg mixture. Shape into balls; roll in additional granulated sugar. Place on ungreased cookie sheet; bake in 375° oven for 10 to 12 minutes. Immediately press a chocolate candy into each. Makes 7 dozen.

CHOCOLATE-CHIP OATMEAL COOKIES

1 cup flour
1 tsp. baking soda
½ tsp. salt
1 stick margarine,
  softened
½ cup shortening
1 cup granulated sugar
½ cup brown sugar, firmly
  packed

2 eggs
½ tsp. vanilla
2¼ cups quick-cooking
  oatmeal
1 (12 oz.) pkg. chocolate
  chips
1 cup chopped nuts,
  (optional)

Sift together flour, baking soda, and salt. Beat margarine, shortening, and sugars together until fluffy. Beat in eggs one at a time; stir in vanilla. Gradually stir in flour. Stir in oatmeal. Then add chocolate chips and nuts. Drop by teaspoonfuls onto lightly greased cookie sheets. Bake in preheated 375° oven 8 to 10 minutes, or until golden. Makes about 6 dozen cookies.

THE WORLD'S EASIEST COOKIES

1 (8 oz.) chocolate bar   2 T. butter
1 sq. bitter chocolate   3 cups cornflakes

Melt chocolate bar, chocolate, and butter in top of double boiler. When melted, add cornflakes and mix. Spoon on waxed paper to dry. No more cooking is required. *Do not make these in hot weather.*

DESSERTS

COCONUT CAKE

½ lb. butter   3 cups all-purpose flour
½ cup shortening   ½ tsp. baking soda
3 cups sugar   Pinch of salt
5 eggs   1 tsp. vanilla
1 cup milk   1 tsp. lemon extract

Cream sugar, butter, and shortening. Add eggs one at a time. Sift flour with baking powder and salt and add alternately with milk. Add flavoring. Mix well, but do not overbeat. Bake in four 9-inch layer pans at 350° for 15 to 20 minutes or until they test done.

Frosting

1½ cups sugar   2 tsp. white corn syrup
⅓ cup cold water   2 egg whites

Mix together and cook in double boiler until mixture holds in peaks.

1 fresh coconut, grated   Coconut juice

Cover layers well with coconut juice, then frosting and as much grated coconut as desired.

WHITE FRUITCAKE

2 lbs. white raisins
2 cups orange juice
5 cups sifted flour
¼ tsp. baking powder
   (if all-purpose flour is used)
½ tsp. salt
1 lb. candied cherries, diced
1 lb. candied pineapple, diced
½ lb. candied citron, diced
¼ lb. candied lemon peel, diced
¼ lb. candied orange peel, diced
1 lb. nuts, chopped fine
1 fresh coconut, grated
2 cups butter or margarine
2¼ cups sugar
6 eggs

Chop raisins (if desired), combine with 1 cup orange juice. Let stand overnight. Sift flour; measure and reserve 2 cups to mix with candied fruits and nuts. Sift remaining 3 cups with baking powder and salt.

Flour candied fruits and nuts separately wth reserved flour.

Cream butter, add sugar, and beat well. Add eggs one at a time, beating well after each addition.

Add sifted flour gradually, beating after each addition. Add coconut, floured fruit and nuts, raisins, and remaining orange juice and beat well.

Bake in two 9- or 10-inch tube pans or several small loaf pans at 250° for 2½ or 3 hours, or until well done. Keep in cool place, wrapped in aluminum foil or in a cake cover. Makes almost 11 lbs. of fruit cake.

COCONUT CAKE

2 cups granulated sugar	2 (12 oz.) pkgs. frozen
2 cups sour cream	coconut

Mix together and leave covered in refrigerator overnight. Bake a yellow cake. Make two layers and split each layer, making four. Ice with mixture between layers and on top—do not ice sides. Seal in cake cover and refrigerate for 4 days. Icing is slightly liquid and is absorbed by cake, which becomes quite moist.

BANANA-SPLIT CAKE

2½ cups graham cracker crumbs	3 bananas
3 sticks margarine	1 large can pineapple
⅔ box powdered sugar	1 large container whipped topping
1 egg	½ cup nuts, chopped
	3 or 4 cherries, chopped

Mix cracker crumbs and 1 stick melted margarine. Crumble in bottom of dish. Mix sugar, egg, and 2 sticks soft margarine. Beat 10 or 15 minutes. Spread on top of crumb mixture. Slice bananas lengthwise and place on top. Add drained pineapple. Top with whipped topping, cherries, and nuts. Refrigerate.

BANANA NUT CAKE

¾ cup shortening	1 tsp. salt
1½ cups sugar	4 T. buttermilk
2 egg yolks	1 tsp. soda
1 cup bananas, mashed	1 T. vanilla
1 tsp. baking powder	2 egg whites, beaten
2 cups flour, sifted	1 cup nuts, chopped

Grease and flour two loaf pans. Cream shortening and sugar, add egg yolks and bananas. Beat well. Add flour, salt, baking powder, buttermilk, vanilla, and soda. Beat well. Fold in egg whites and nuts. Bake one hour at 325°.

STRAWBERRY LAYER CAKE

        1 box white cake mix
        1 sm. pkg. strawberry gelatin
        1 cup oil
        1 cup frozen strawberries
        ½ cup milk
        4 eggs
        1 cup flaked coconut
        1 cup nuts

Mix and bake in 3 layers at 350° for 25 or 30 minutes.

Frosting

1 box powdered sugar   ½ cup nuts
1 stick margarine   ½ cup coconut
½ cup strawberries

Mix together and spread on thoroughly cooled cake.

PIG-PICKIN' CAKE

1 box yellow cake mix   ¾ cup oil
4 eggs   1 (11 oz.) can undrained
                              Mandarin oranges

Combine above and mix well with electric mixer. Pour into
9-inch cake pans for 4 layers, or into 10-inch pans for 3
layers. Bake at 350° for 15 minutes.

Icing

        1 lg. can crushed pineapple, very slightly drained
        1 (9 oz.) container whipped topping
        1 (3 oz.) pkg. instant vanilla pudding

Mix pineapple with pudding mix and blend well. Fold in
whipped topping and spread on thoroughly cooled cake.

GRAHAM-CRACKER CAKE

½ cup butter
2 cups sugar
5 eggs
1 cup milk

1 cup coconut
2 tsps. baking powder
2 tsps. vanilla extract
1 lb. box graham crackers

Crush graham crackers. Mix all ingredients thoroughly. Bake in three layers at 300 to 350° for 35 to 40 minutes.

Icing

1 box confectioner's sugar
1 stick butter or margarine
1 large can crushed pineapple, drained

Ice three layers with these ingredients creamed well together. Add nuts if desired.

NEVER FAIL PIE CRUST

3 cups flour
½ tsp. salt
¼ cup sugar
1 egg

1¼ cups shortening
1 T. vinegar
3 T. water

EASY CHOCOLATE OR LEMON PIE

1 cup sugar
½ stick butter or
  margarine
3 T. cocoa

2 T. milk
1 tsp. vanilla
2 whole eggs

Melt butter and sugar together. Stir in cocoa and milk. Add eggs and mix well. Pour into unbaked pie crust and bake at 350° for 30 minutes.

Variation: Substitute juice and rind of 2 lemons for cocoa.

OLD-FASHIONED LEMON PIE

½ stick butter, melted
1 cup sugar
3 eggs, separated

Juice of 2 lemons
Grated rind of 1 lemon, if
  tart; if not, 2 lemons

Beat egg yolks until thick; gradually add sugar. Add lemon juice, rind, and melted butter. Beat egg whites into light peaks (not too stiff); fold into other mixture. Mix thoroughly. Pour into baked pie shell. Bake at 350° until light brown.

LEMON PIES (2)

Juice and rind of 2
  lemons
3 T. butter
3 cups boiling water

4 eggs, separated
2½ cups sugar
6 heaping T. flour
2 baked pie shells

Mix all ingredients except egg whites and cook, stirring constantly, until thick. Pour into pie shells. Beat egg whites with a pinch of cream of tartar or salt until stiff. Add 8 T. sugar, two at a time, beating each addition thoroughly. Spread on pies and bake at 350° until brown—about 15 minutes.

PECAN PIES (2)

3 eggs, beaten
1 cup granulated sugar
1 cup dark corn syrup
1 tsp. vanilla

Pinch salt
¼ stick butter, melted
1 tsp. corn meal
1 cup pecans, chopped

Mix dry ingredients. Add eggs and other ingredients, adding pecans last. Pour into unbaked pie shell. Preheat oven to 300° and bake for 45 to 50 minutes.

SOUR CREAM PIE

1 cup sour cream	1 tsp. cinnamon
¾ cup sugar	½ tsp. nutmeg
½ tsp. ground cloves	2 eggs, slightly beaten
Pinch salt	½ cup pecans

Mix sugar and sour cream together. Add eggs and remaining ingredients. Pour into unbaked pie shell and bake at 425° for 20 minutes. Reduce heat to 325° and bake for 20 minutes more. Top with sweetened whipped cream and pecans.

One cup undiluted evaporated milk, plus 1 T. vinegar, may be used in place of sour cream.

IMPOSSIBLE PIE

4 eggs	2 cups milk
1¾ cups sugar	1 (7 oz.) pkg. flaked
½ stick margarine,	coconut
softened	1 tsp. vanilla
½ cup self-rising flour	

Beat eggs; add other ingredients in order listed. Pour into two well-greased pie pans. Bake at 350° for 35 to 40 minutes.

THREE-THING PIE

1 frozen graham cracker crust
1 extra large chocolate bar with almonds
1 large container whipped topping

Melt chocolate bar in top of double boiler. Fold in whipped topping, stirring well. Pour into pie shell and chill for one hour or longer.

CHERRY-TOPPED CHEESE PIE

1 (8 oz.) pkg. cream
  cheese, softened
½ cup sugar
2 cups whipped topping

1 (9 in.) graham cracker
  crust
1 cup cherry pie filling

Beat together cream cheese and sugar until creamy. Blend in whipped topping. Pour into unbaked graham cracker crust. Top with cherry pie filling. Chill 3 hours before serving.

HURRY PIES (2)

2 graham cracker crusts
1 can sweetened
  condensed milk
1 lg. can crushed
  pineapple

Juice of 2 lemons
1 (9 oz.) container whipped
  topping

Mix milk and lemon juice. Add crushed pineapple. Fold in whipped topping. Spoon into pie shells and chill at least 30 minutes before serving.

    Frozen strawberries or other fruit may be substituted for pineapple.

CHIFFON PIES (2)

    1 cup pineapple juice, unsweetened
    ½ cup sugar
    1 sm. pkg. lemon gelatin (or any flavor)
    1 can evaporated milk
    2 graham cracker or vanilla wafer pie shells

Freeze evaporated milk. Bring pineapple juice and sugar to a boil. Remove from heat and dissolve gelatin in liquid. Refrigerate until partly thickened.

    Whip milk with electric mixer and add gelatin mixture. Pour into pie crusts and chill.

STRAWBERRY PIE

1 baked pie shell	3 T. cornstarch
3 T. strawberry gelatin	1 cup sugar
1 cup boiling water	Whipped cream or whipped
Fresh strawberries	topping

Bring water to boil in saucepan. Mix gelatin, cornstarch, and sugar together and add slowly to water. Cook for several minutes, until thick. Set aside to cool.

Clean and halve strawberries. Arrange in pie shell and pour sauce over them. Chill. Top with whipped cream or whipped topping.

BANANA-SPLIT SUNDAE PIE

1 graham cracker pie crust	Whipped cream or whipped topping
1 quart strawberry ice cream, softened	Pecans, chopped
Maraschino cherries	2 small ripe bananas

Spoon half softened ice cream into crust, smoothing top. Split bananas lengthwise and arrange spoke-style on ice cream. Spoon remaining ice cream over bananas, swirling the top. Freeze until firm, about 2 hours. Decorate with whipped cream, pecans and cherries.

LEMON BISQUE

Graham cracker crumbs	⅔ cup sugar
1 can evaporated milk	Juice and some rind of 2 lemons

Chill milk, then beat with mixer until it thickens. Add sugar gradually. Add lemon juice and rind. Line glass dish with graham cracker crumbs. Pour milk mixture on crumbs and sprinkle top with graham crackers. Freeze.

BUTTER BRICKLE ICE-CREAM PIE & SAUCE

Pie
9-inch graham cracker pie shell
½ gallon vanilla ice cream, softened
About 4 oz. butterscotch bits or crushed toffee or
      caramel candy

Spoon half of softened ice cream into prepared pie shell.
Sprinkle bits of candy on top. Heap with remaining ice
cream. Freeze.

Sauce

1½ cups sugar	¼ cup butter or margarine
1 cup evaporated milk	¼ cup light corn syrup
About 4 oz. butterscotch	Dash salt
bits or crushed candies	

Combine sugar, milk, butter or margarine, syrup and salt.
Bring to boil over low heat; boil 1 minute. Remove from
heat and stir in remaining bits or candy. Cool, stirring
occasionally. Chill. To serve, stir sauce well, spoon over
individual pie wedges.

STRAWBERRY DESSERT

2 pkgs. strawberry gelatin
1½ cups hot water
1 cup cold water
1 cup sweetened whipped cream or 1 pint whipped
      topping
2 pkgs. frozen strawberries, thawed
1 large angelfood cake

Prepare gelatin as directed on package with hot and cold
water. Refrigerate until slightly thickened. Break angelfood cake into chunks. Toss together with gelatin, whipped
cream or topping, and strawberries.

MISSISSIPPI MUD

2 sticks margarine,
  melted
2 cups sugar
½ tsp. salt
1½ cups nuts

½ cup cocoa
4 eggs, well beaten
1½ cups all-purpose flour
½ tsp. vanilla
1 pkg. miniature
  marshmallows

Mix well and press into 10 X 13 pan. Bake at 350° for 30 minutes. Top with marshmallows, return to oven and toast slightly. Drizzle with chocolate icing.

Icing

    ½ stick margarine
    ½ cup milk
    ⅓ cup cocoa
    1 tsp. vanilla
    1 box powdered sugar

Combine margarine, milk, and cocoa in saucepan. When margarine is melted, add vanilla. Beat in sugar.

BANANA TORTE

1 cup graham crackers, crushed
3 T. butter, melted
1 (15 oz.) can sweetened condensed milk
½ cup lemon juice
2 ripe bananas, diced (peaches may be used)
1 T. sugar
1 cup heavy cream, whipped, or whipped topping

Combine cracker crumbs and butter. Reserve 2 T. of the crumb mixture. Press remaining crumbs evenly over bottom of lightly buttered pan. Add ⅓ cup lemon juice to milk and blend well or until thick. Mix lightly together bananas, remaining lemon juice, and sugar. Fold into milk mixture. Fold in whipped cream or topping and pour into pan. Spread evenly. Chill until firm.

DANISH PUFF

1 cup flour, sifted   ½ cup butter
½ cup butter or margarine   1 cup water
2 T. water   1 tsp. almond flavoring
                                         1 cup flour, sifted
                                         3 eggs

Heat oven to 350°. Measure first cup of flour into bowl; cut
in butter or margarine; sprinkle with 2 T. water; mix with
fork. Round into ball and divide in half. Pat dough into two
long strips 12 X 3 inches, 3 inches apart, on ungreased
baking sheet. Mix the second amount of butter and water;
bring to a rolling boil; add almond flavoring and remove
from heat. Stir in flour immediately to keep from lumping;
when smooth and thick, add 1 egg at a time, beating until
smooth. Divide in half and spread each half evenly over
each piece of pastry.

Bake for about 60 minutes until topping is crisp and
nicely browned. Frost with confectioners' sugar icing and
sprinkle with chopped nuts and/or coconut. *Note:* Must be
served the day you make it!!

BEVERAGES

LIME PUNCH

1 (3 oz.) pkg. lime gelatin   1 (8 oz.) bottle concentrated
2 cups sugar   lemon juice
2 large cans pineapple   2 bottles ginger ale
   juice

Mix gelatin with 2 cups boiling water. Combine all
ingredients except ginger ale and add enough water to
make 1 gallon. Freeze. Remove from freezer about 6 hours
before ready to serve. Chip and add ginger ale. It will be
like slush; no ice needed.

COLD CRANBERRY PUNCH

4 cups cranberry juice
1½ cups sugar
2 qts. ginger ale

4 cups pineapple juice, unsweetened
1 T. almond extract

Combine all ingredients except ginger ale. Chill. Add chilled ginger ale before serving.

WEDDING RECEPTION PUNCH

2 (26 oz.) cans fruit-flavored punch, chilled
1 (6 oz.) can frozen limeade concentrate, thawed
1 (6 oz.) can frozen lemonade concentrate, thawed
2 (28 oz.) bottles club soda, chilled
Lemon and lime slices

In a very large punch bowl, combine canned punch and limeade and lemonade concentrates. Stir until well blended. Just before serving, stir in club soda. Add citrus slices and ice cubes.

INSTANT RUSSIAN TEA

1 medium size jar instant orange drink
½ cup instant tea
1½ cups sugar

1 tsp. ground cloves
1 tsp. ground cinnamon

Shake ingredients together in large jar. Use 2 tsp. of mix to 1 cup hot water.

INSTANT HOT CHOCOLATE MIX

6 cups instant nonfat dry milk
1 (3 oz.) jar powdered creamer
1 (16 oz.) can instant chocolate drink mix
1 cup powdered sugar

Mix thoroughly and store in airtight container. Use 2 to 3 T. mix to 1 cup hot water.

SHIRLEY TEMPLE

1 bottle carbonated lemon/lime beverage
1 T. grenadine syrup
1 T. cherry juice
2 T. orange juice (a little fresh squeezed)
Sugar (about 1 tsp. per bottle lemon/lime
  beverage)

BIBLIOGRAPHY

Anderson, Doris. *The Encyclopedia of Games.* Grand Rapids: Zondervan, 1955.

Burns, Lorell Coffman. *Instant Party Fun.* New York: Associated Press, 1967.

Carlson, Adelle. *Four Seasons Party and Banquet Book.* Nashville: Broadman Press, 1965.

Holbert, Joe. *Word Party and Banquet Book.* Waco, Tex.: Word Books, 1980.

Richart, Genevieve. *The Master Game and Party Book.* Grand Rapids: Baker Book House, 1973.

Sessoms, Bob, and Sessoms, Carolyn. *52 Complete Recreation Programs for Senior Adults.* Nashville: Convention Press, 1979.

Smith, Frank Hart. *Fellowships: Plenty of Fun for All.* Nashville: Convention Press, 1978.

Smith, Frank Hart. *52 Complete After-Game Fellowships.* Nashville: Convention Press, 1980.

Smith, Frank Hart. *Social Recreation and the Church.* Nashville: Convention Press, 1977.

Wade, Mildred. *Socials for All Occasions.* Nashville: Broadman Press, 1980.

INDEX